nickelodeon™

降击神通

AVATAR

THE LAST AIRBENDER™

Created by
Bryan Konietzko
Michael Dante DiMartino

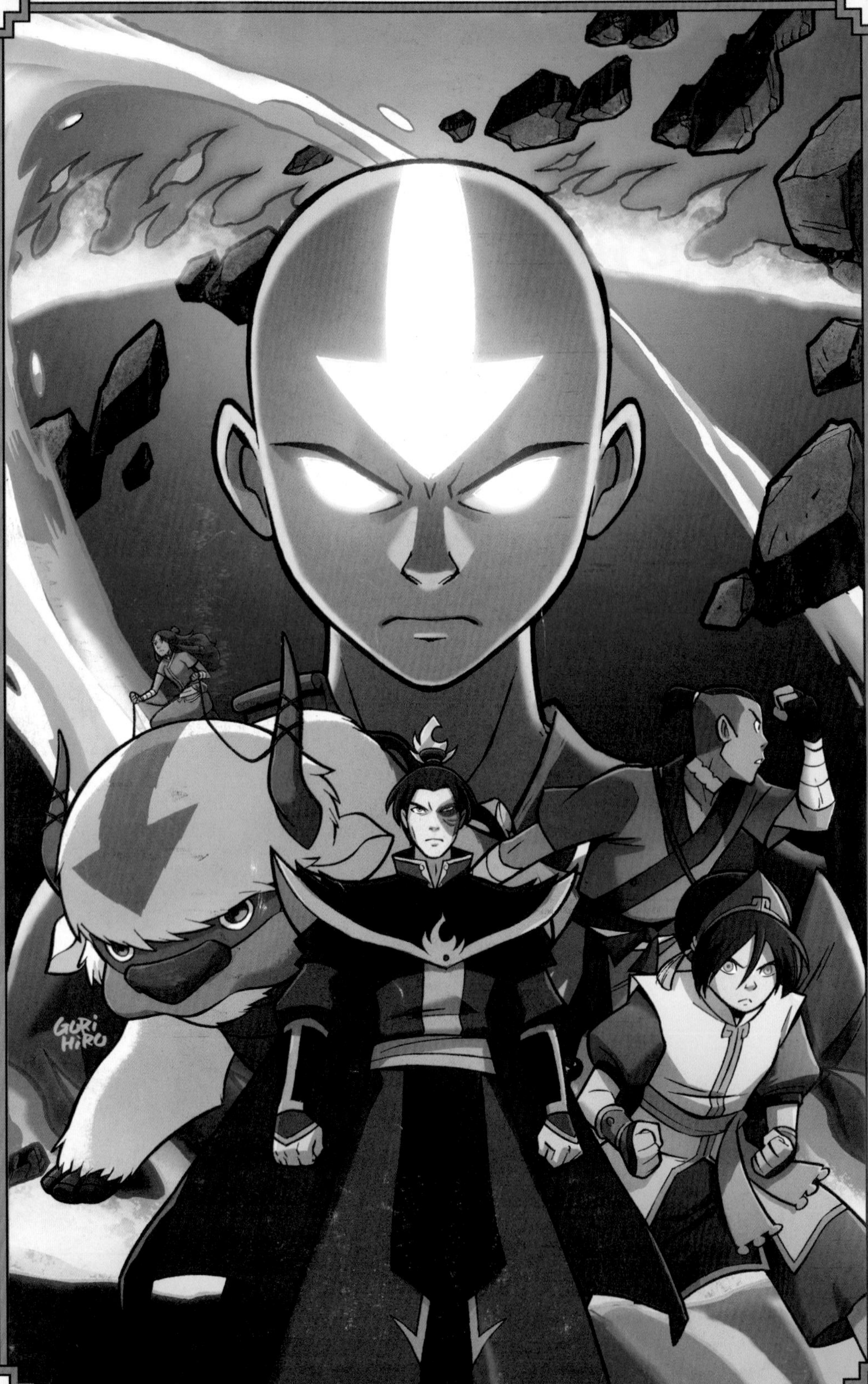
GURI HIRU

nickelodeon

降击神通

AVATAR

THE LAST AIRBENDER

THE PROMISE · PART THREE

script
GENE LUEN YANG

art and cover
GURIHIRU

lettering
MICHAEL HEISLER

DARK HORSE BOOKS

publisher
MIKE RICHARDSON

designer
JUSTIN COUCH

assistant editor
BRENDAN WRIGHT

editor
DAVE MARSHALL

Special thanks to Linda Lee, Kat van Dam, James Salerno,
and Joan Hilty at Nickelodeon, to Samantha Robertson,
and to Bryan Konietzko and Michael Dante DiMartino.

Published by
Dark Horse Books
A division of
Dark Horse Comics, Inc.
10956 SE Main Street
Milwaukie, OR 97222

DarkHorse.com
Nick.com

To find a comics shop in your area, call the Comic Shop
Locator Service toll-free at (888) 266-4226.

First edition: September 2012
ISBN 978-1-59582-941-2

1 3 5 7 9 10 8 6 4 2
Printed in the United States of America

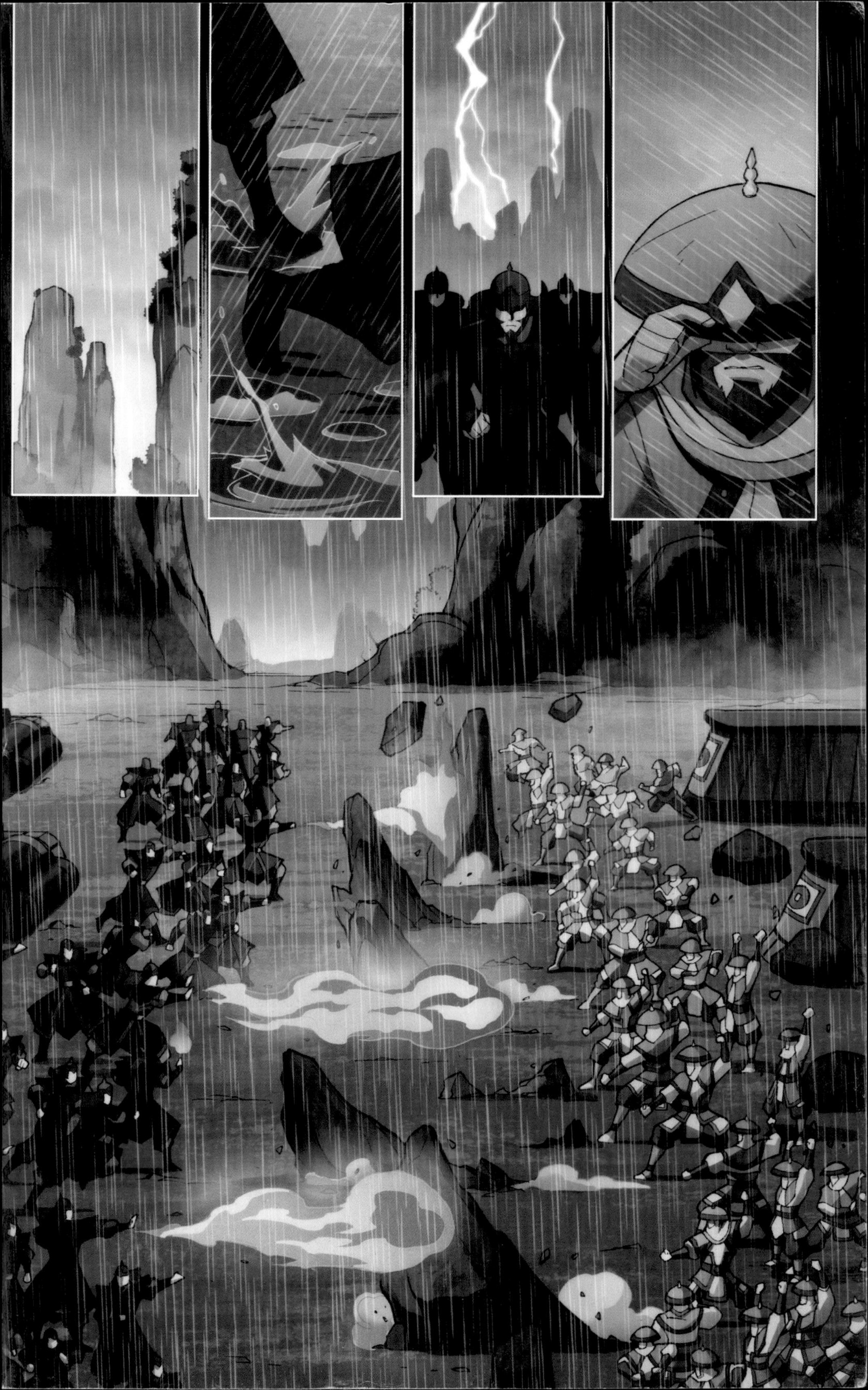

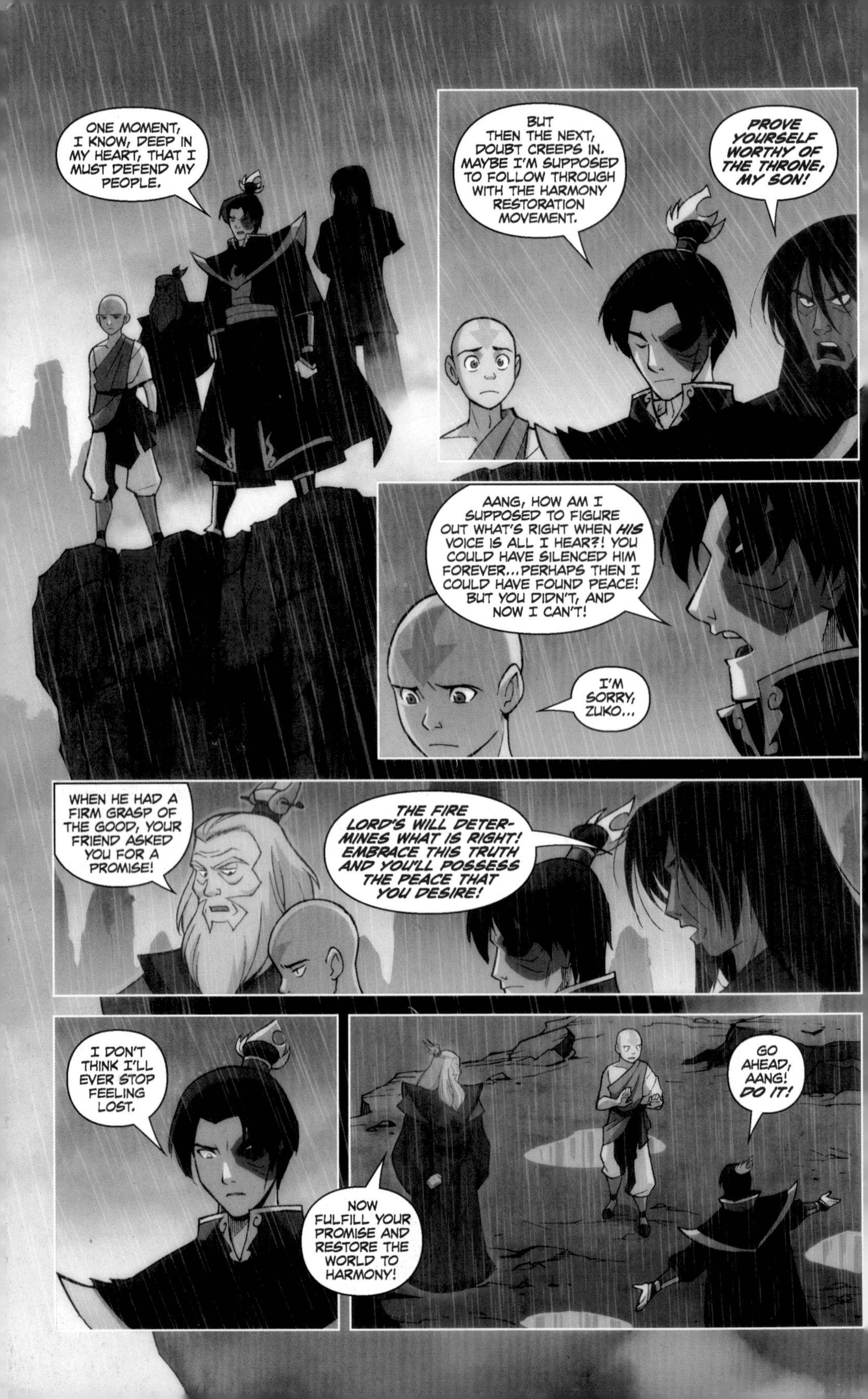
ONE MOMENT, I KNOW, DEEP IN MY HEART, THAT I MUST DEFEND MY PEOPLE.
BUT THEN THE NEXT, DOUBT CREEPS IN. MAYBE I'M SUPPOSED TO FOLLOW THROUGH WITH THE HARMONY RESTORATION MOVEMENT.
PROVE YOURSELF WORTHY OF THE THRONE, MY SON!
AANG, HOW AM I SUPPOSED TO FIGURE OUT WHAT'S RIGHT WHEN HIS VOICE IS ALL I HEAR?! YOU COULD HAVE SILENCED HIM FOREVER...PERHAPS THEN I COULD HAVE FOUND PEACE! BUT YOU DIDN'T, AND NOW I CAN'T!
I'M SORRY, ZUKO...
WHEN HE HAD A FIRM GRASP OF THE GOOD, YOUR FRIEND ASKED YOU FOR A PROMISE!
THE FIRE LORD'S WILL DETERMINES WHAT IS RIGHT! EMBRACE THIS TRUTH AND YOU'LL POSSESS THE PEACE THAT YOU DESIRE!
I DON'T THINK I'LL EVER STOP FEELING LOST.
NOW FULFILL YOUR PROMISE AND RESTORE THE WORLD TO HARMONY!
GO AHEAD, AANG! DO IT!

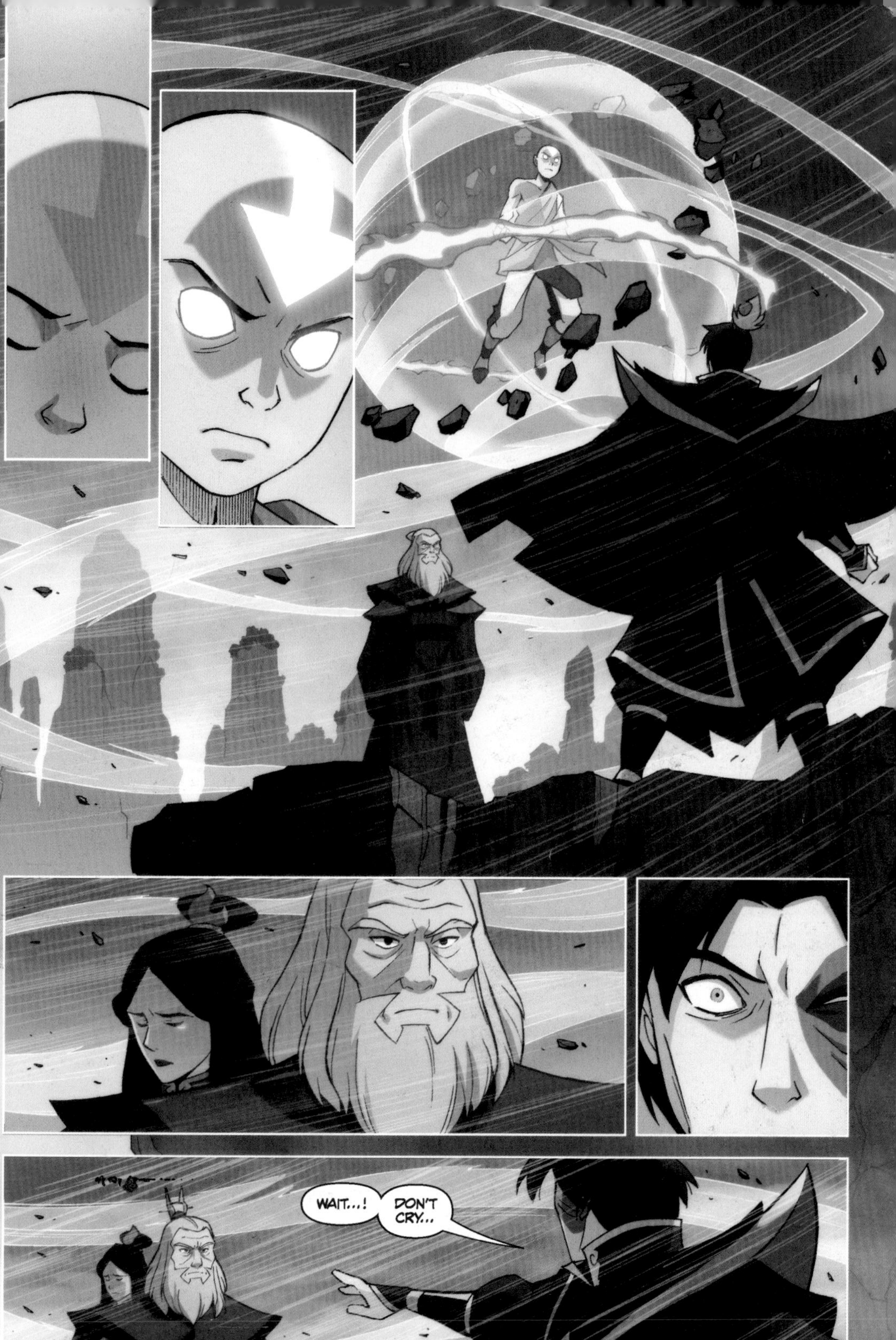

WAIT...!
DON'T CRY...

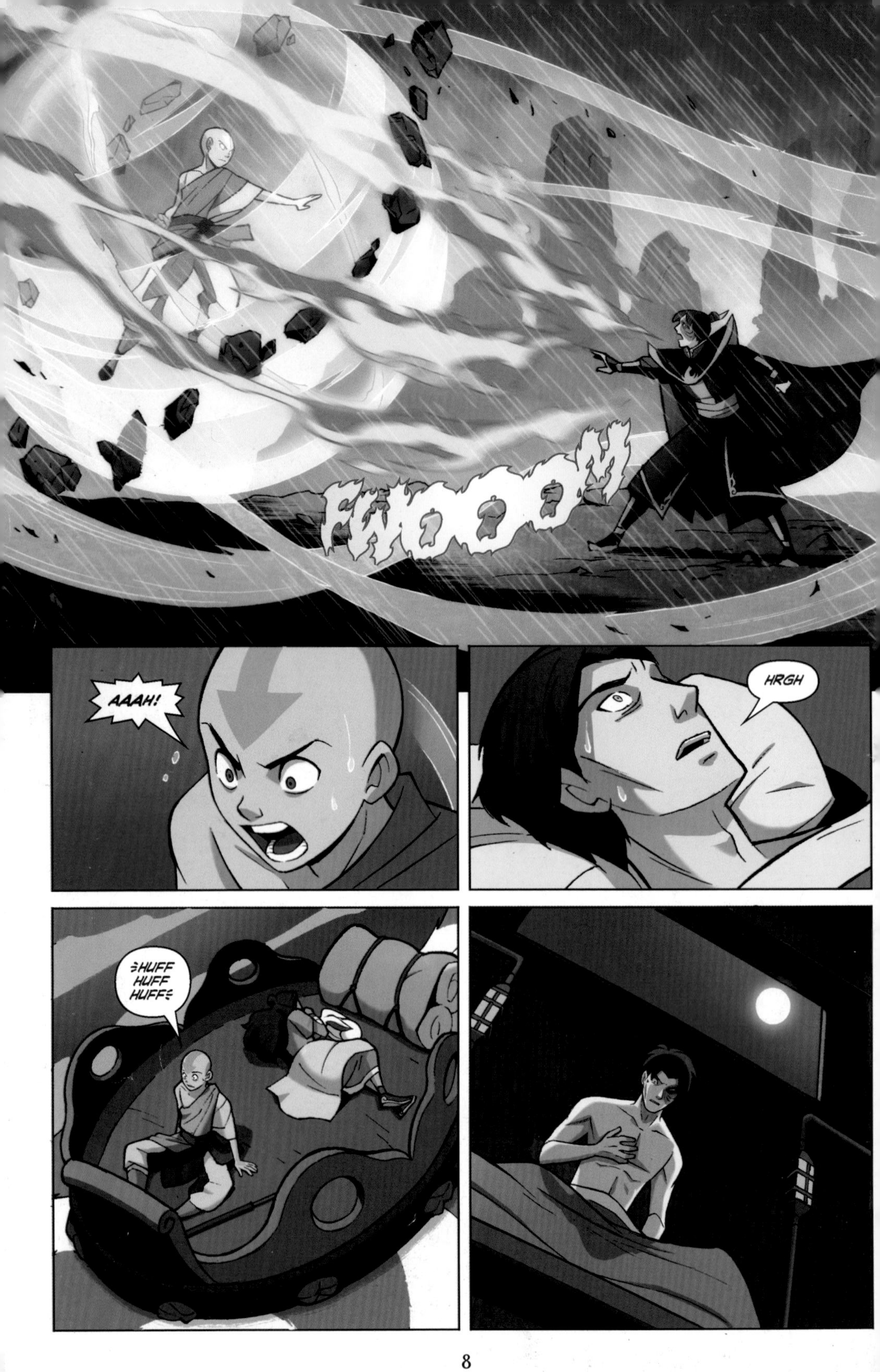
FWOOOM
AAAH!
HRGH
HUFF
HUFF
HUFF

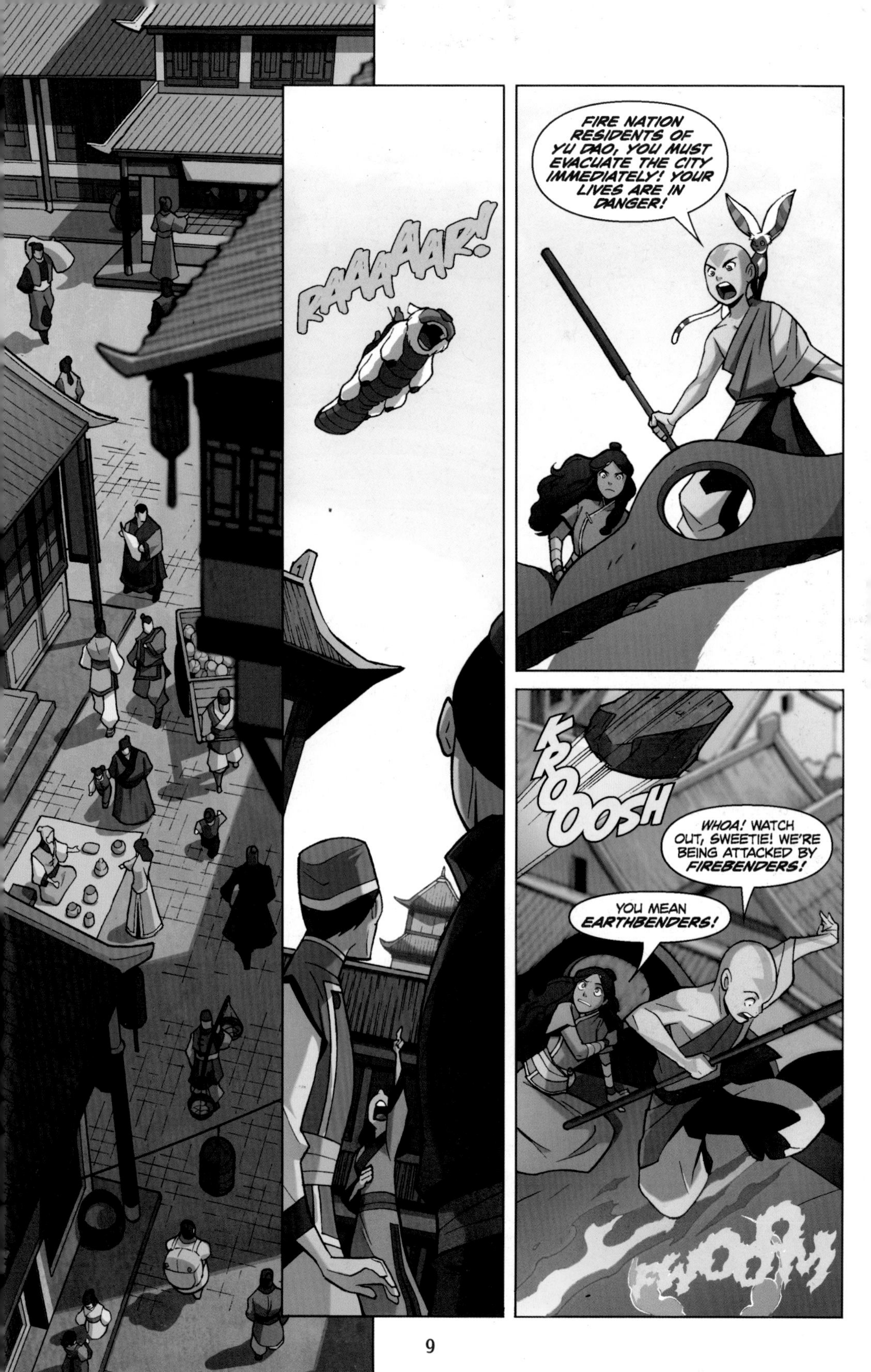
RAAAAAR!
FIRE NATION RESIDENTS OF YU DAO, YOU MUST EVACUATE THE CITY IMMEDIATELY! YOUR LIVES ARE IN DANGER!
KROOOOSH
WHOA! WATCH OUT, SWEETIE! WE'RE BEING ATTACKED BY FIREBENDERS!
YOU MEAN EARTHBENDERS!
FWOOM

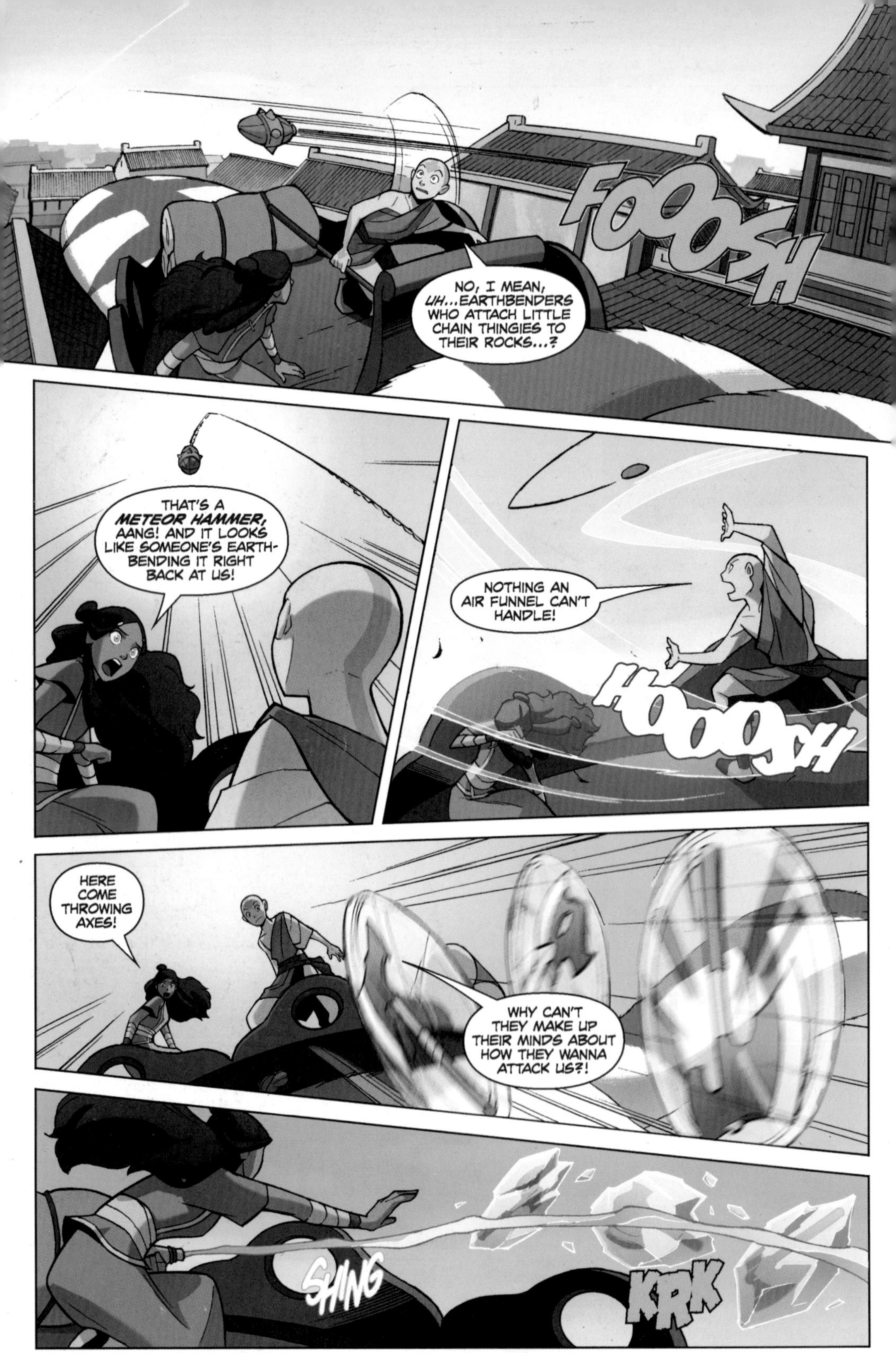
NO, I MEAN, UH...EARTHBENDERS WHO ATTACH LITTLE CHAIN THINGIES TO THEIR ROCKS...?
FOOOSH
THAT'S A METEOR HAMMER, AANG! AND IT LOOKS LIKE SOMEONE'S EARTH-BENDING IT RIGHT BACK AT US!
NOTHING AN AIR FUNNEL CAN'T HANDLE!
HOOOSH
HERE COME THROWING AXES!
WHY CAN'T THEY MAKE UP THEIR MINDS ABOUT HOW THEY WANNA ATTACK US?!
SHING
KRK

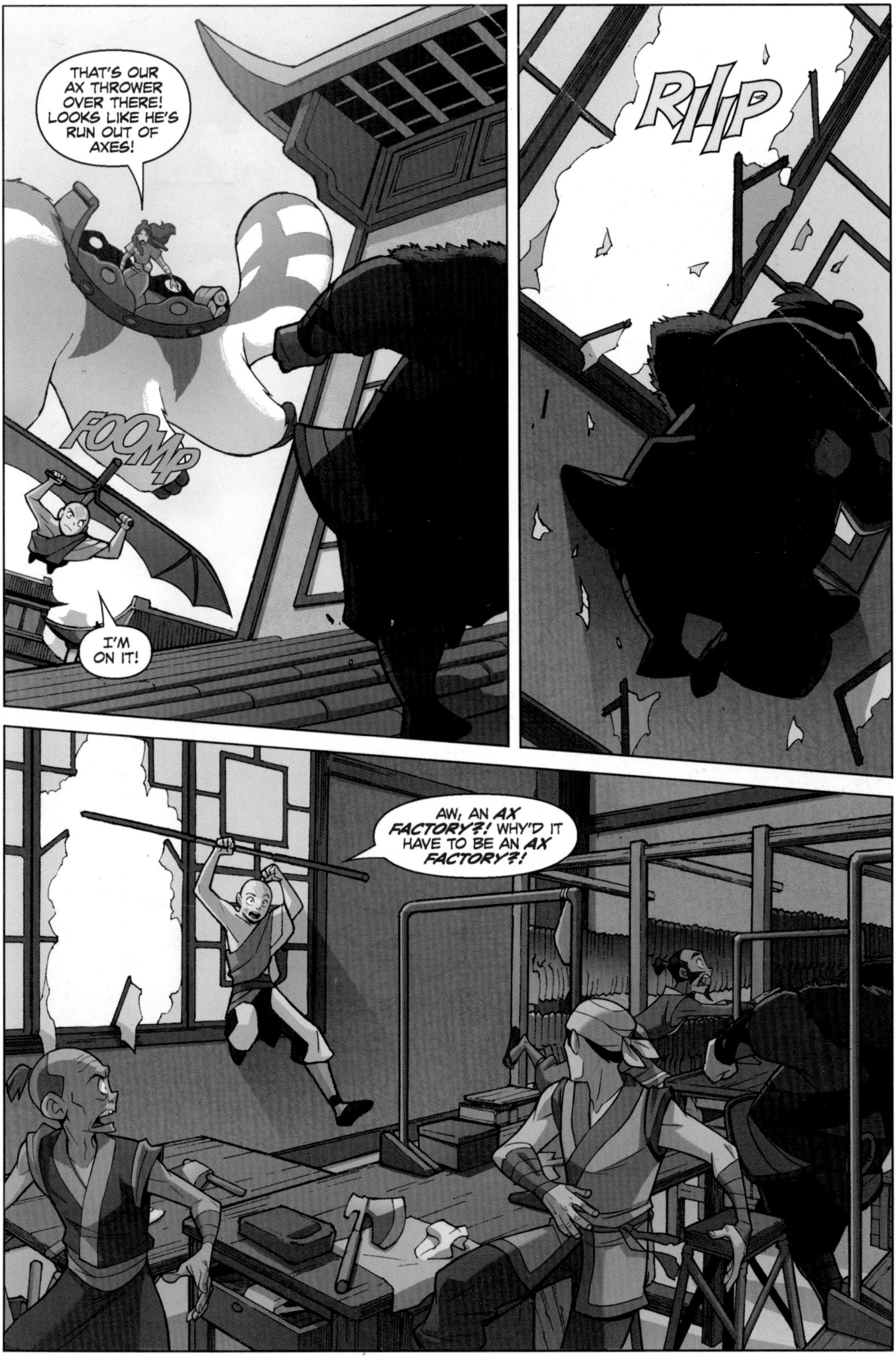
THAT'S OUR AX THROWER OVER THERE! LOOKS LIKE HE'S RUN OUT OF AXES!
FOOMP
I'M ON IT!
RIIIP
AW, AN AX FACTORY?! WHY'D IT HAVE TO BE AN AX FACTORY?!

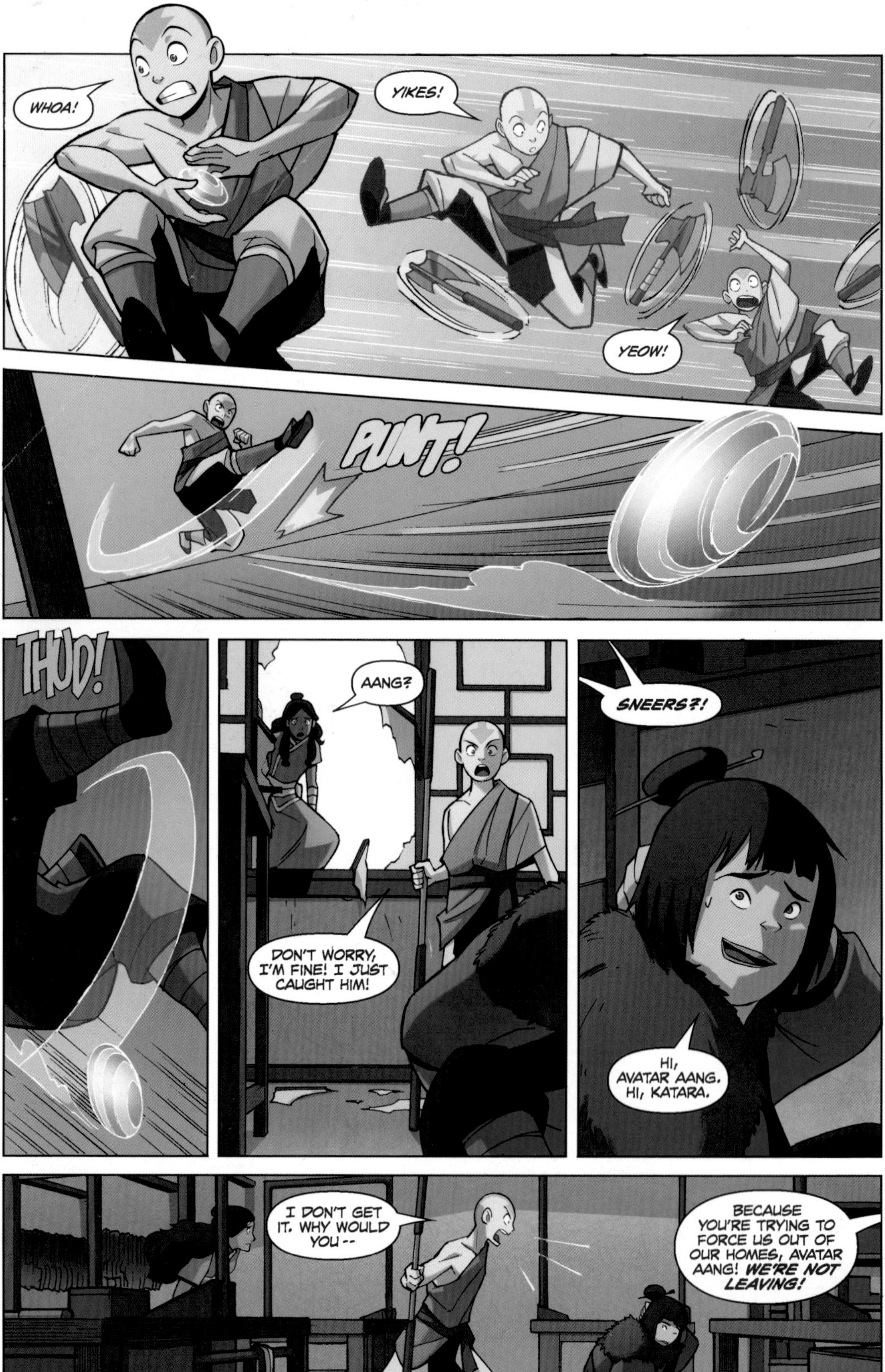
WHOA!
YIKES!
YEOW!
PUNT!
THUD!
AANG?
DON'T WORRY, I'M FINE! I JUST CAUGHT HIM!
SNEERS?!
HI, AVATAR AANG. HI, KATARA.
I DON'T GET IT. WHY WOULD YOU --
BECAUSE YOU'RE TRYING TO FORCE US OUT OF OUR HOMES, AVATAR AANG! WE'RE NOT LEAVING!

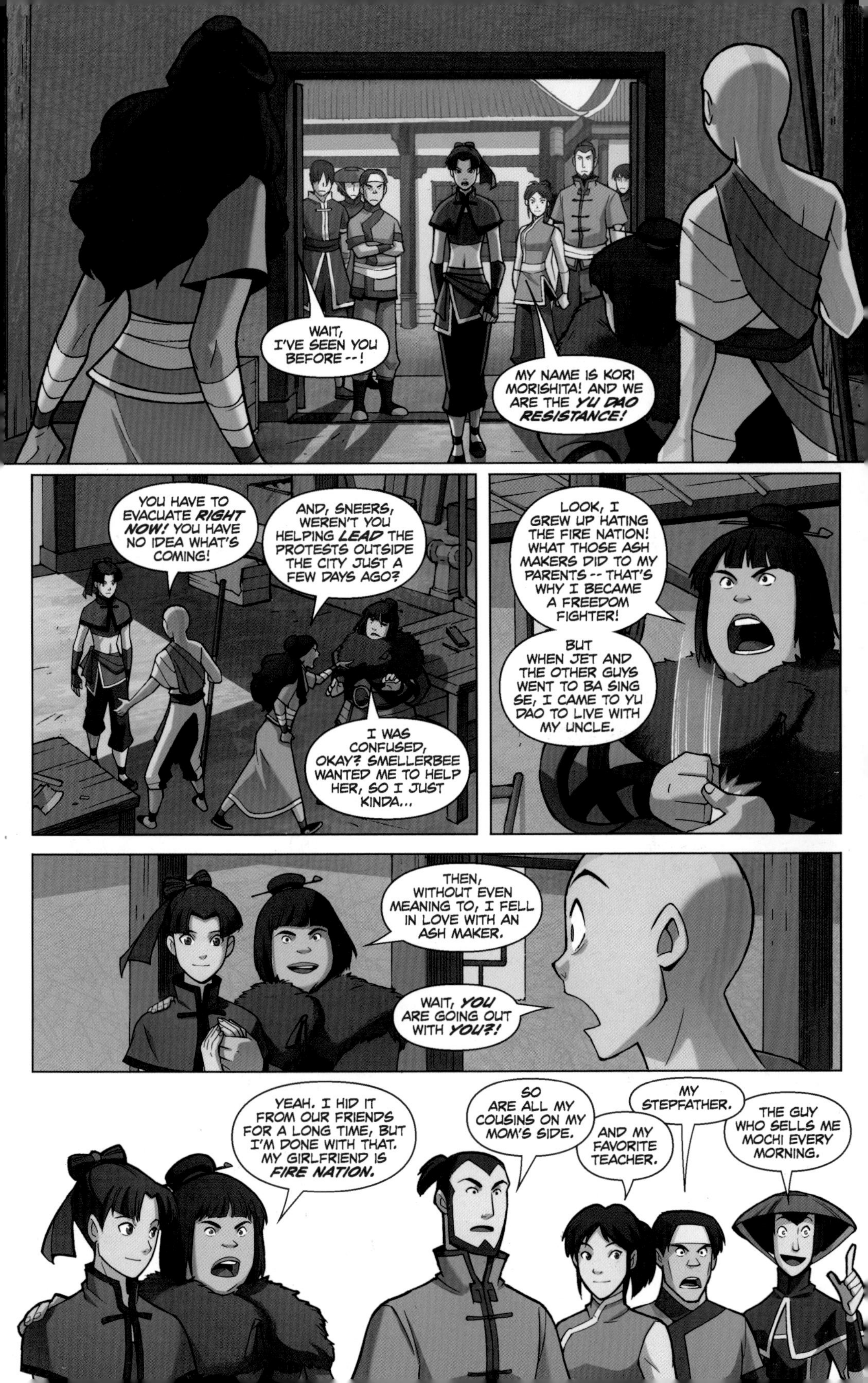
WAIT, I'VE SEEN YOU BEFORE--!
MY NAME IS KORI MORISHITA! AND WE ARE THE YU DAO RESISTANCE!
YOU HAVE TO EVACUATE RIGHT NOW! YOU HAVE NO IDEA WHAT'S COMING!
AND, SNEERS, WEREN'T YOU HELPING LEAD THE PROTESTS OUTSIDE THE CITY JUST A FEW DAYS AGO?
I WAS CONFUSED, OKAY? SMELLERBEE WANTED ME TO HELP HER, SO I JUST KINDA...
LOOK, I GREW UP HATING THE FIRE NATION! WHAT THOSE ASH MAKERS DID TO MY PARENTS -- THAT'S WHY I BECAME A FREEDOM FIGHTER!
BUT WHEN JET AND THE OTHER GUYS WENT TO BA SING SE, I CAME TO YU DAO TO LIVE WITH MY UNCLE.
THEN, WITHOUT EVEN MEANING TO, I FELL IN LOVE WITH AN ASH MAKER.
WAIT, YOU ARE GOING OUT WITH YOU?!
YEAH. I HID IT FROM OUR FRIENDS FOR A LONG TIME, BUT I'M DONE WITH THAT. MY GIRLFRIEND IS FIRE NATION.
SO ARE ALL MY COUSINS ON MY MOM'S SIDE.
AND MY FAVORITE TEACHER.
MY STEPFATHER.
THE GUY WHO SELLS ME MOCHI EVERY MORNING.

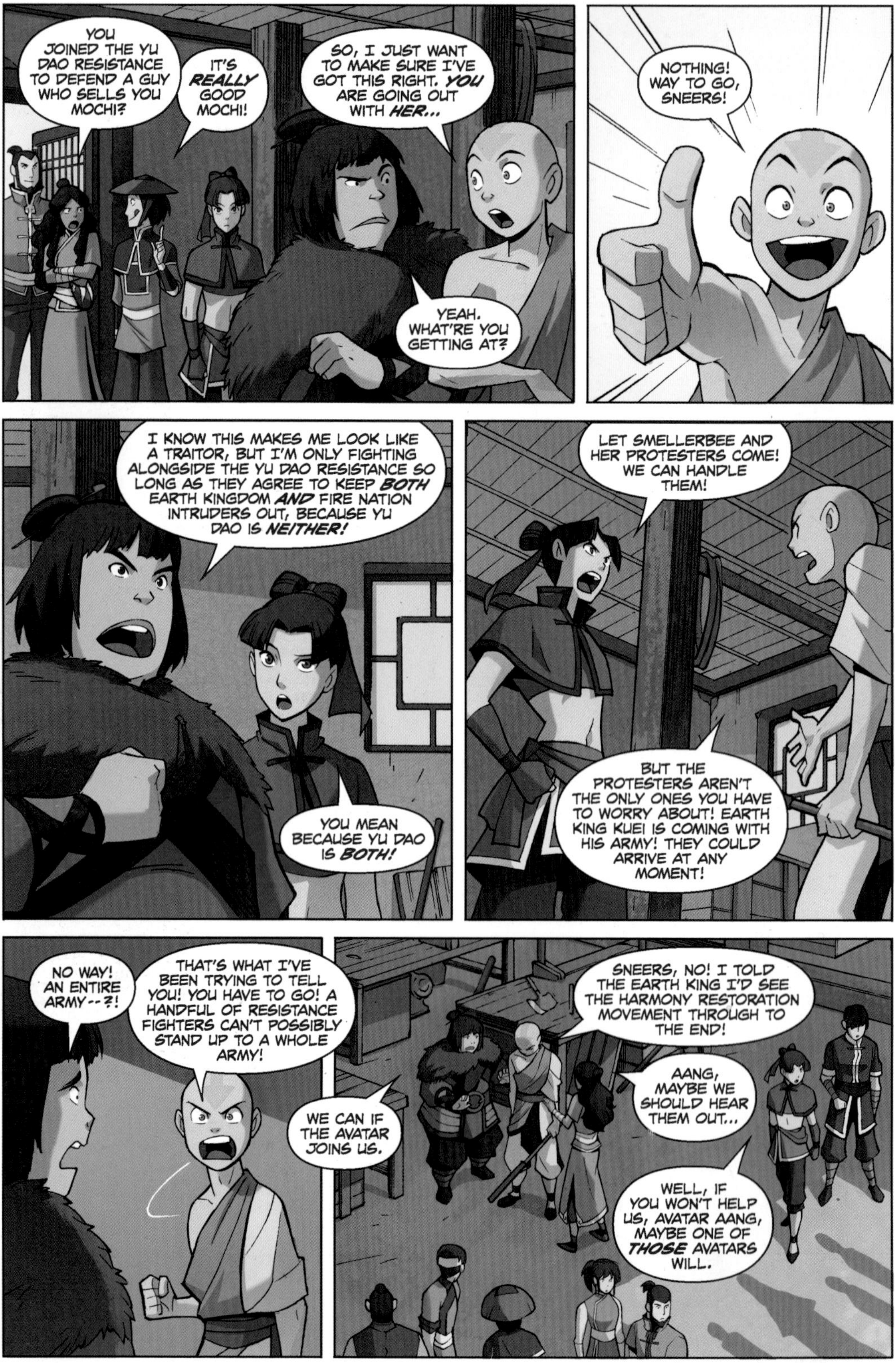
YOU JOINED THE YU DAO RESISTANCE TO DEFEND A GUY WHO SELLS YOU MOCHI?
IT'S REALLY GOOD MOCHI!
SO, I JUST WANT TO MAKE SURE I'VE GOT THIS RIGHT. YOU ARE GOING OUT WITH HER...
YEAH. WHAT'RE YOU GETTING AT?
NOTHING! WAY TO GO, SNEERS!
I KNOW THIS MAKES ME LOOK LIKE A TRAITOR, BUT I'M ONLY FIGHTING ALONGSIDE THE YU DAO RESISTANCE SO LONG AS THEY AGREE TO KEEP BOTH EARTH KINGDOM AND FIRE NATION INTRUDERS OUT, BECAUSE YU DAO IS NEITHER!
YOU MEAN BECAUSE YU DAO IS BOTH!
LET SMELLERBEE AND HER PROTESTERS COME! WE CAN HANDLE THEM!
BUT THE PROTESTERS AREN'T THE ONLY ONES YOU HAVE TO WORRY ABOUT! EARTH KING KUEI IS COMING WITH HIS ARMY! THEY COULD ARRIVE AT ANY MOMENT!
NO WAY! AN ENTIRE ARMY--?!
THAT'S WHAT I'VE BEEN TRYING TO TELL YOU! YOU HAVE TO GO! A HANDFUL OF RESISTANCE FIGHTERS CAN'T POSSIBLY STAND UP TO A WHOLE ARMY!
WE CAN IF THE AVATAR JOINS US.
SNEERS, NO! I TOLD THE EARTH KING I'D SEE THE HARMONY RESTORATION MOVEMENT THROUGH TO THE END!
AANG, MAYBE WE SHOULD HEAR THEM OUT...
WELL, IF YOU WON'T HELP US, AVATAR AANG, MAYBE ONE OF THOSE AVATARS WILL.

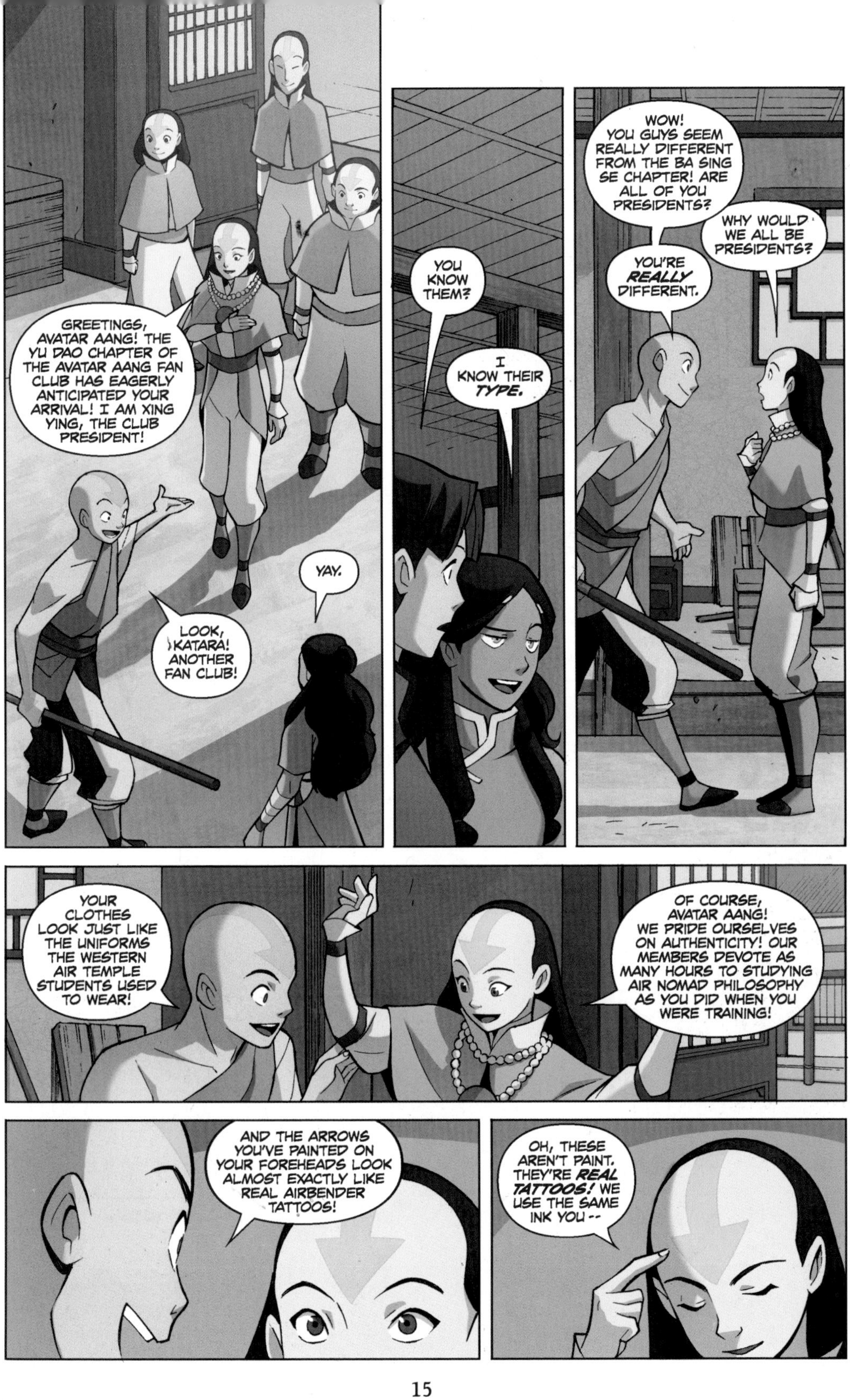
GREETINGS, AVATAR AANG! THE YU DAO CHAPTER OF THE AVATAR AANG FAN CLUB HAS EAGERLY ANTICIPATED YOUR ARRIVAL! I AM XING YING, THE CLUB PRESIDENT!
LOOK, KATARA! ANOTHER FAN CLUB!
YAY.
YOU KNOW THEM?
I KNOW THEIR *TYPE.*
WOW! YOU GUYS SEEM REALLY DIFFERENT FROM THE BA SING SE CHAPTER! ARE ALL OF YOU PRESIDENTS?
WHY WOULD WE ALL BE PRESIDENTS?
YOU'RE *REALLY* DIFFERENT.
YOUR CLOTHES LOOK JUST LIKE THE UNIFORMS THE WESTERN AIR TEMPLE STUDENTS USED TO WEAR!
OF COURSE, AVATAR AANG! WE PRIDE OURSELVES ON AUTHENTICITY! OUR MEMBERS DEVOTE AS MANY HOURS TO STUDYING AIR NOMAD PHILOSOPHY AS YOU DID WHEN YOU WERE TRAINING!
AND THE ARROWS YOU'VE PAINTED ON YOUR FOREHEADS LOOK ALMOST EXACTLY LIKE REAL AIRBENDER TATTOOS!
OH, THESE AREN'T PAINT. THEY'RE *REAL TATTOOS!* WE USE THE SAME INK YOU --

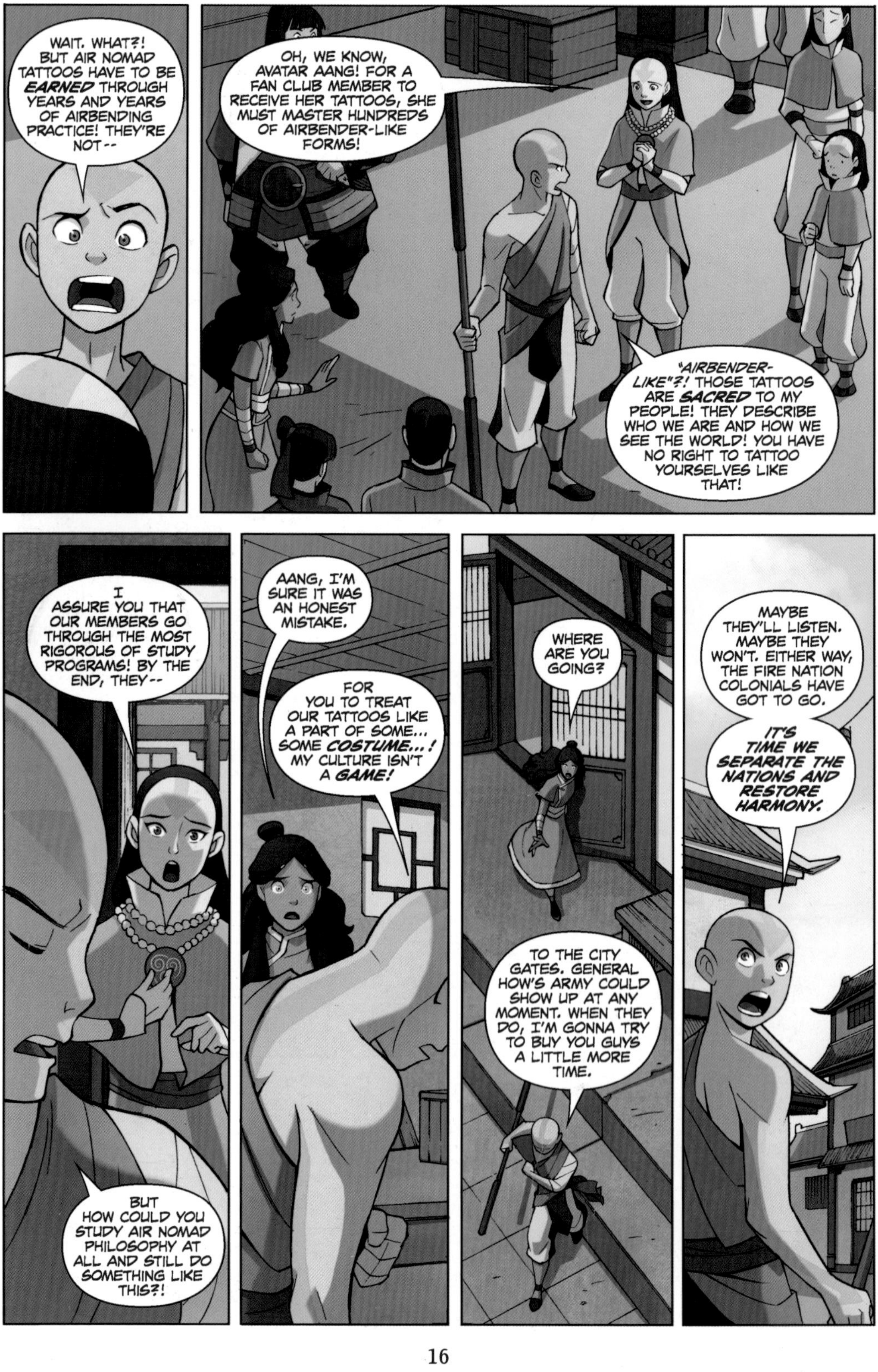
WAIT. WHAT?! BUT AIR NOMAD TATTOOS HAVE TO BE *EARNED* THROUGH YEARS AND YEARS OF AIRBENDING PRACTICE! THEY'RE NOT--
OH, WE KNOW, AVATAR AANG! FOR A FAN CLUB MEMBER TO RECEIVE HER TATTOOS, SHE MUST MASTER HUNDREDS OF AIRBENDER-LIKE FORMS!
"AIRBENDER-LIKE"?! THOSE TATTOOS ARE *SACRED* TO MY PEOPLE! THEY DESCRIBE WHO WE ARE AND HOW WE SEE THE WORLD! YOU HAVE NO RIGHT TO TATTOO YOURSELVES LIKE THAT!
I ASSURE YOU THAT OUR MEMBERS GO THROUGH THE MOST RIGOROUS OF STUDY PROGRAMS! BY THE END, THEY--
BUT HOW COULD YOU STUDY AIR NOMAD PHILOSOPHY AT ALL AND STILL DO SOMETHING LIKE THIS?!
AANG, I'M SURE IT WAS AN HONEST MISTAKE.
FOR YOU TO TREAT OUR TATTOOS LIKE A PART OF SOME... SOME *COSTUME...!* MY CULTURE ISN'T A *GAME!*
WHERE ARE YOU GOING?
TO THE CITY GATES. GENERAL HOW'S ARMY COULD SHOW UP AT ANY MOMENT. WHEN THEY DO, I'M GONNA TRY TO BUY YOU GUYS A LITTLE MORE TIME.
MAYBE THEY'LL LISTEN. MAYBE THEY WON'T. EITHER WAY, THE FIRE NATION COLONIALS HAVE GOT TO GO.
IT'S TIME WE SEPARATE THE NATIONS AND RESTORE HARMONY.

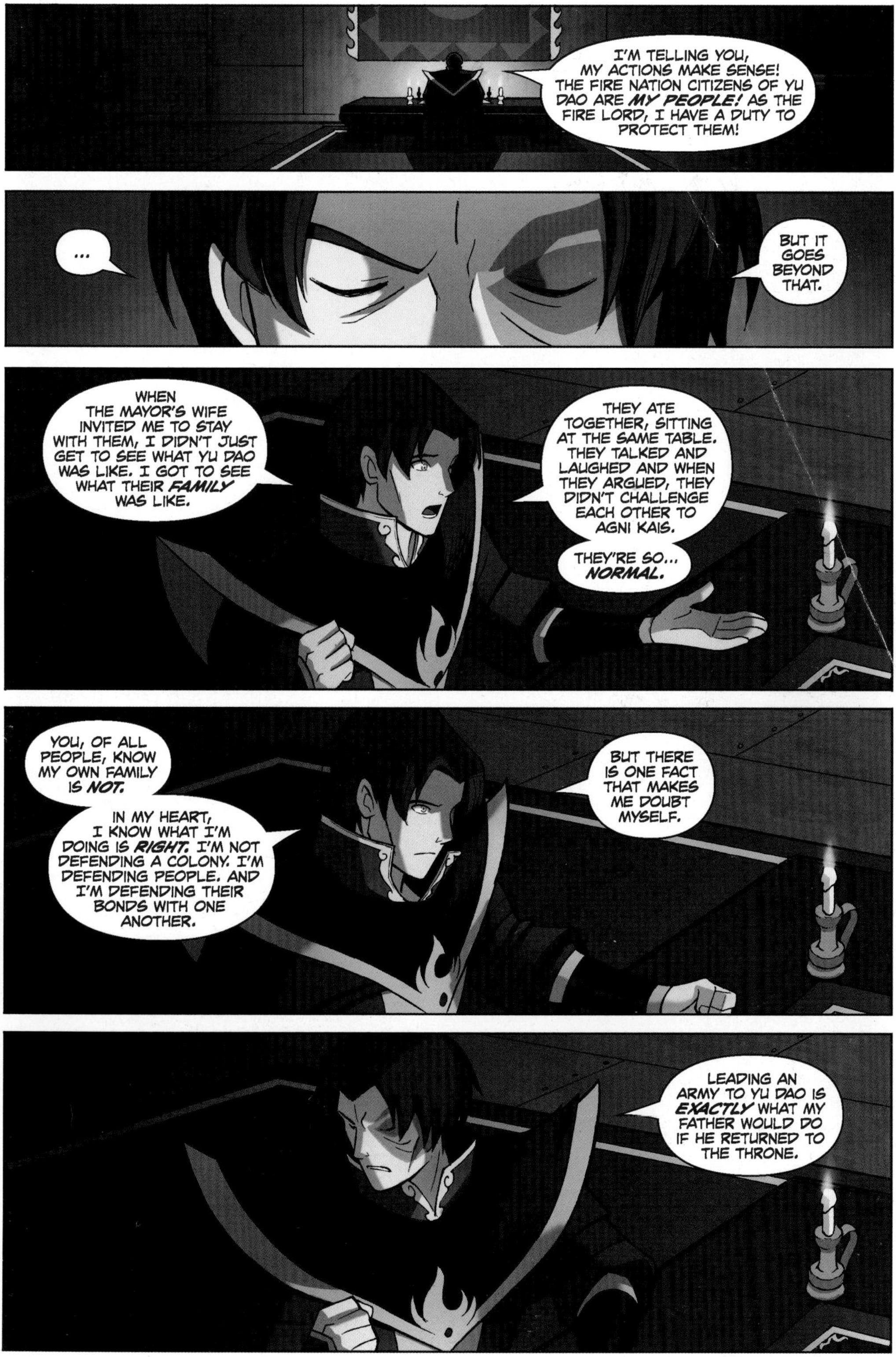
I'M TELLING YOU, MY ACTIONS MAKE SENSE! THE FIRE NATION CITIZENS OF YU DAO ARE ***MY PEOPLE!*** AS THE FIRE LORD, I HAVE A DUTY TO PROTECT THEM!
...
BUT IT GOES BEYOND THAT.
WHEN THE MAYOR'S WIFE INVITED ME TO STAY WITH THEM, I DIDN'T JUST GET TO SEE WHAT YU DAO WAS LIKE. I GOT TO SEE WHAT THEIR ***FAMILY*** WAS LIKE.
THEY ATE TOGETHER, SITTING AT THE SAME TABLE. THEY TALKED AND LAUGHED AND WHEN THEY ARGUED, THEY DIDN'T CHALLENGE EACH OTHER TO AGNI KAIS.
THEY'RE SO... ***NORMAL.***
YOU, OF ALL PEOPLE, KNOW MY OWN FAMILY IS ***NOT.***
IN MY HEART, I KNOW WHAT I'M DOING IS ***RIGHT.*** I'M NOT DEFENDING A COLONY. I'M DEFENDING PEOPLE. AND I'M DEFENDING THEIR BONDS WITH ONE ANOTHER.
BUT THERE IS ONE FACT THAT MAKES ME DOUBT MYSELF.
LEADING AN ARMY TO YU DAO IS ***EXACTLY*** WHAT MY FATHER WOULD DO IF HE RETURNED TO THE THRONE.

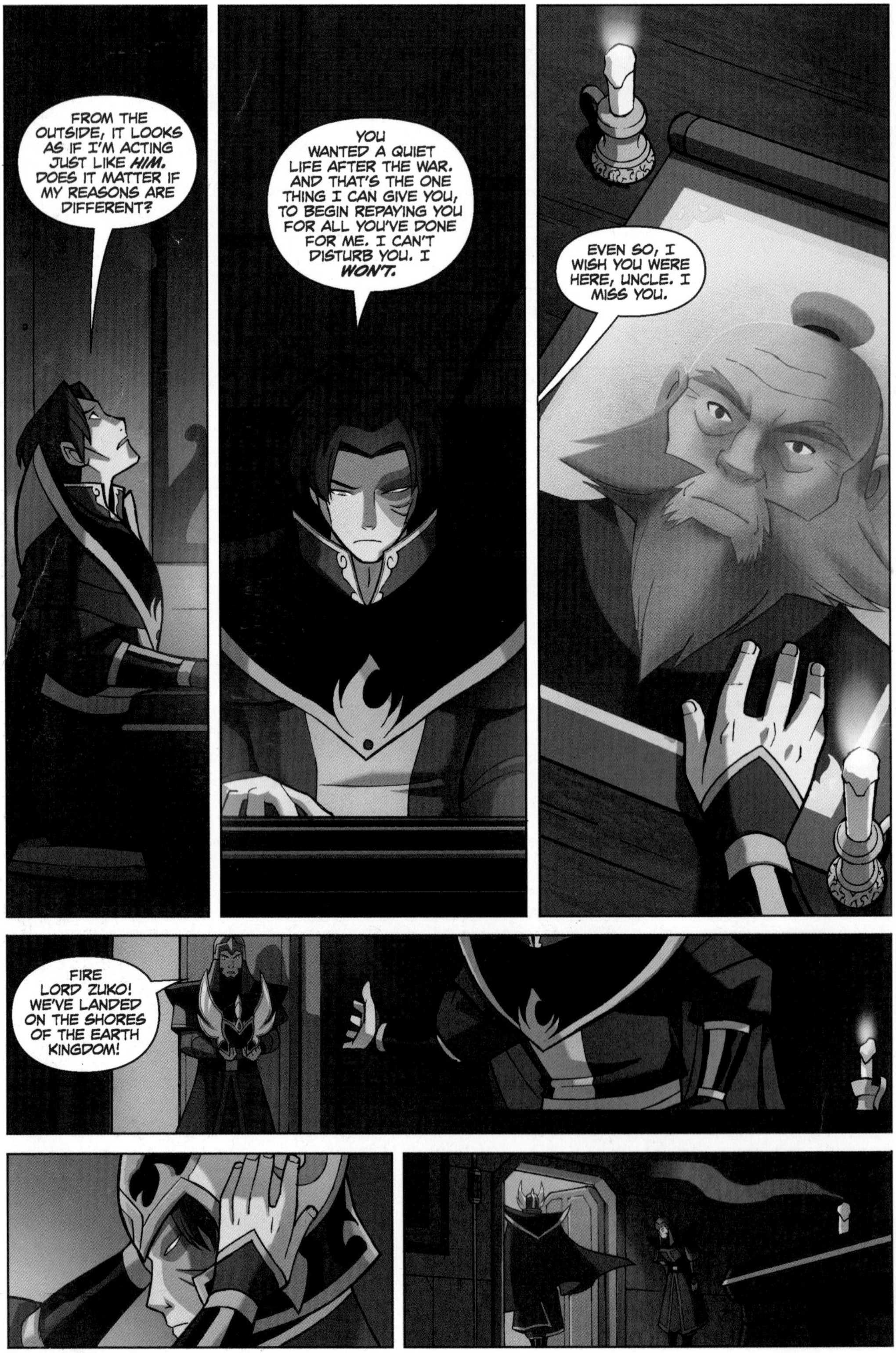
FROM THE OUTSIDE, IT LOOKS AS IF I'M ACTING JUST LIKE *HIM.* DOES IT MATTER IF MY REASONS ARE DIFFERENT?
YOU WANTED A QUIET LIFE AFTER THE WAR. AND THAT'S THE ONE THING I CAN GIVE YOU, TO BEGIN REPAYING YOU FOR ALL YOU'VE DONE FOR ME. I CAN'T DISTURB YOU. I *WON'T.*
EVEN SO, I WISH YOU WERE HERE, UNCLE. I MISS YOU.
FIRE LORD ZUKO! WE'VE LANDED ON THE SHORES OF THE EARTH KINGDOM!

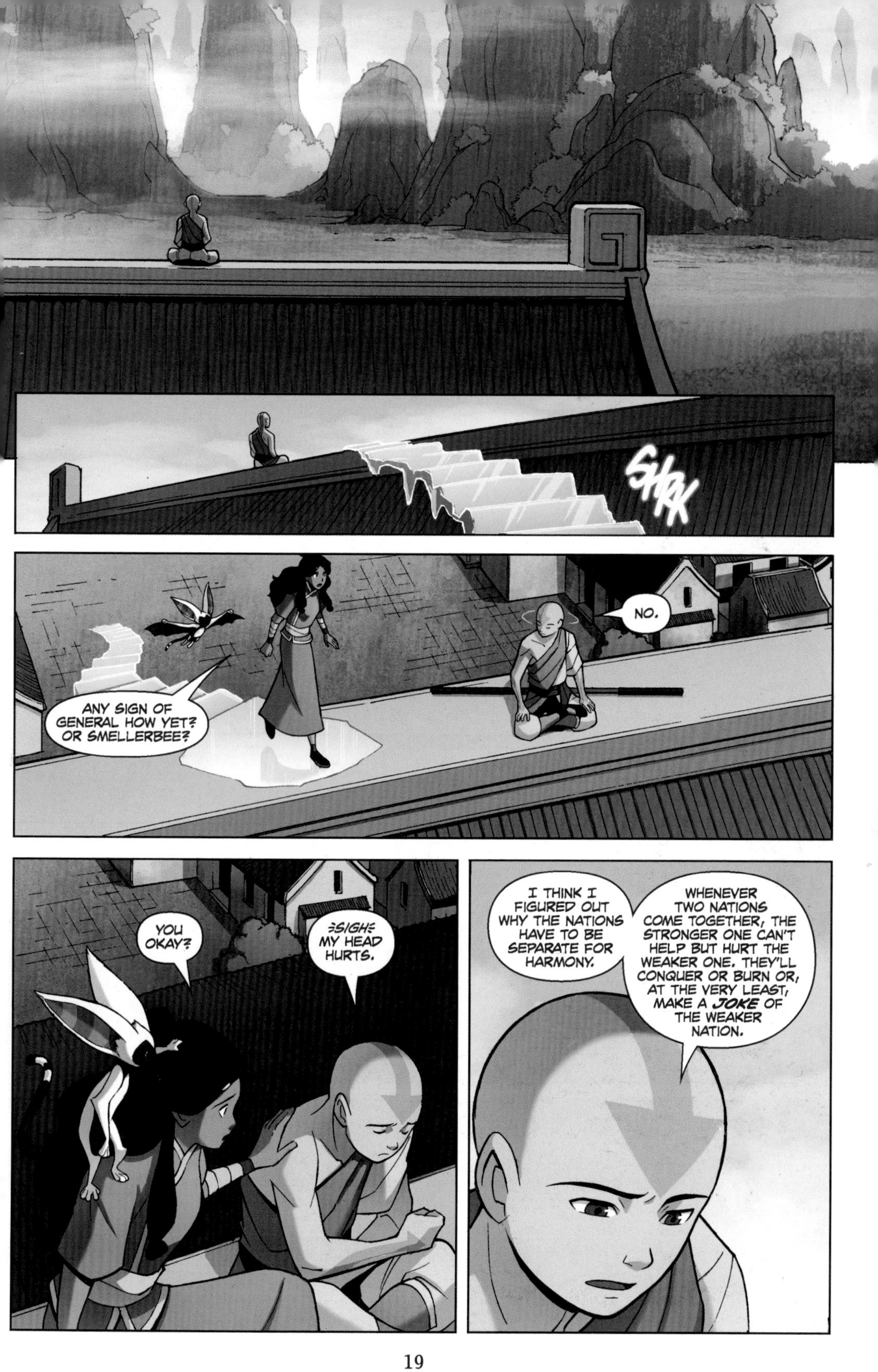
SHRAK
ANY SIGN OF GENERAL HOW YET? OR SMELLERBEE?
NO.
YOU OKAY?
SIGH MY HEAD HURTS.
I THINK I FIGURED OUT WHY THE NATIONS HAVE TO BE SEPARATE FOR HARMONY.
WHENEVER TWO NATIONS COME TOGETHER, THE STRONGER ONE CAN'T HELP BUT HURT THE WEAKER ONE. THEY'LL CONQUER OR BURN OR, AT THE VERY LEAST, MAKE A JOKE OF THE WEAKER NATION.

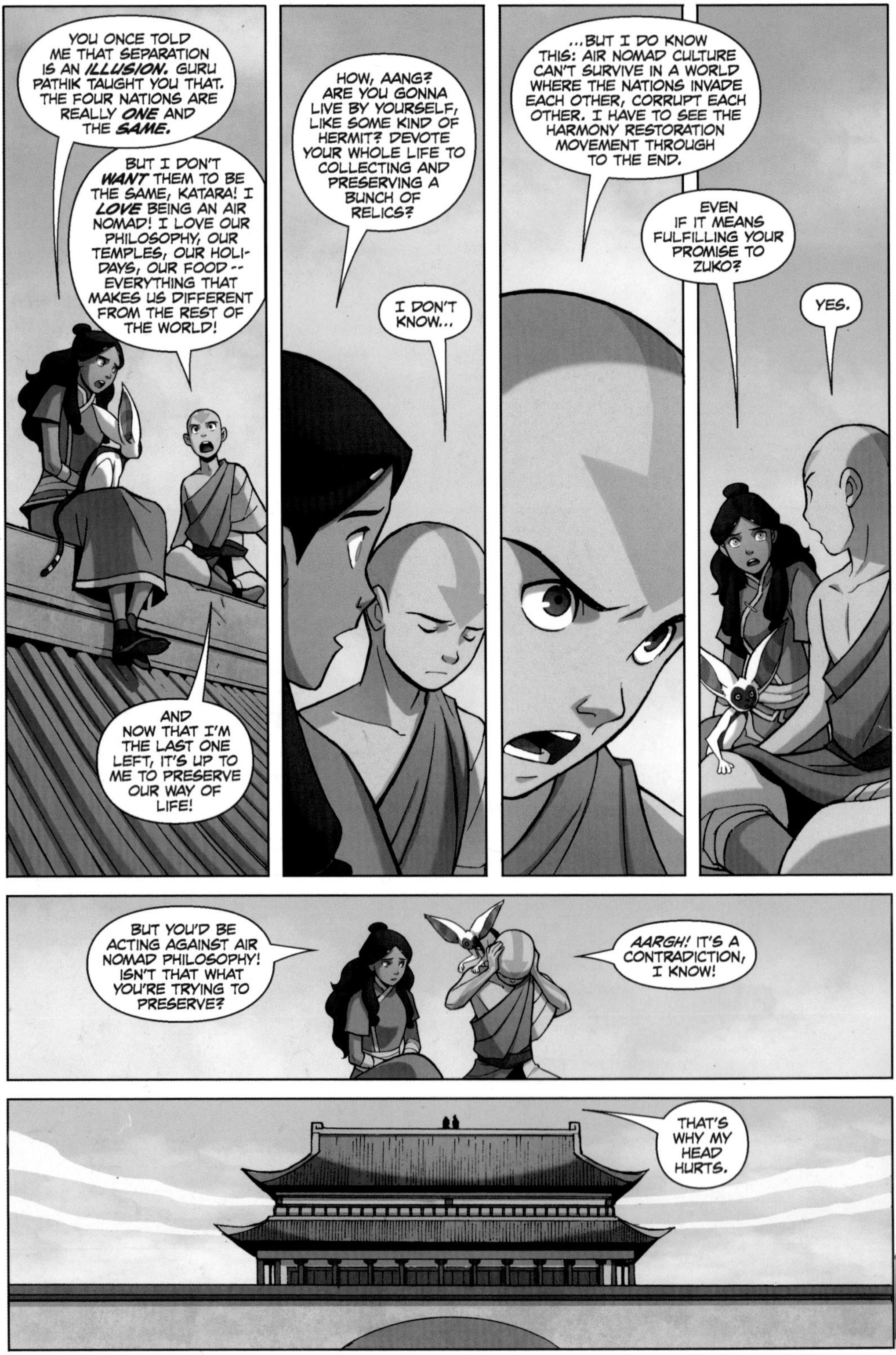
YOU ONCE TOLD ME THAT SEPARATION IS AN *ILLUSION.* GURU PATHIK TAUGHT YOU THAT. THE FOUR NATIONS ARE REALLY *ONE* AND THE *SAME.*
BUT I DON'T *WANT* THEM TO BE THE SAME, KATARA! I *LOVE* BEING AN AIR NOMAD! I LOVE OUR PHILOSOPHY, OUR TEMPLES, OUR HOLI-DAYS, OUR FOOD -- EVERYTHING THAT MAKES US DIFFERENT FROM THE REST OF THE WORLD!
AND NOW THAT I'M THE LAST ONE LEFT, IT'S UP TO ME TO PRESERVE OUR WAY OF LIFE!
HOW, AANG? ARE YOU GONNA LIVE BY YOURSELF, LIKE SOME KIND OF HERMIT? DEVOTE YOUR WHOLE LIFE TO COLLECTING AND PRESERVING A BUNCH OF RELICS?
I DON'T KNOW...
...BUT I DO KNOW THIS: AIR NOMAD CULTURE CAN'T SURVIVE IN A WORLD WHERE THE NATIONS INVADE EACH OTHER, CORRUPT EACH OTHER. I HAVE TO SEE THE HARMONY RESTORATION MOVEMENT THROUGH TO THE END.
EVEN IF IT MEANS FULFILLING YOUR PROMISE TO ZUKO?
YES.
BUT YOU'D BE ACTING AGAINST AIR NOMAD PHILOSOPHY! ISN'T THAT WHAT YOU'RE TRYING TO PRESERVE?
AARGH! IT'S A CONTRADICTION, I KNOW!
THAT'S WHY MY HEAD HURTS.

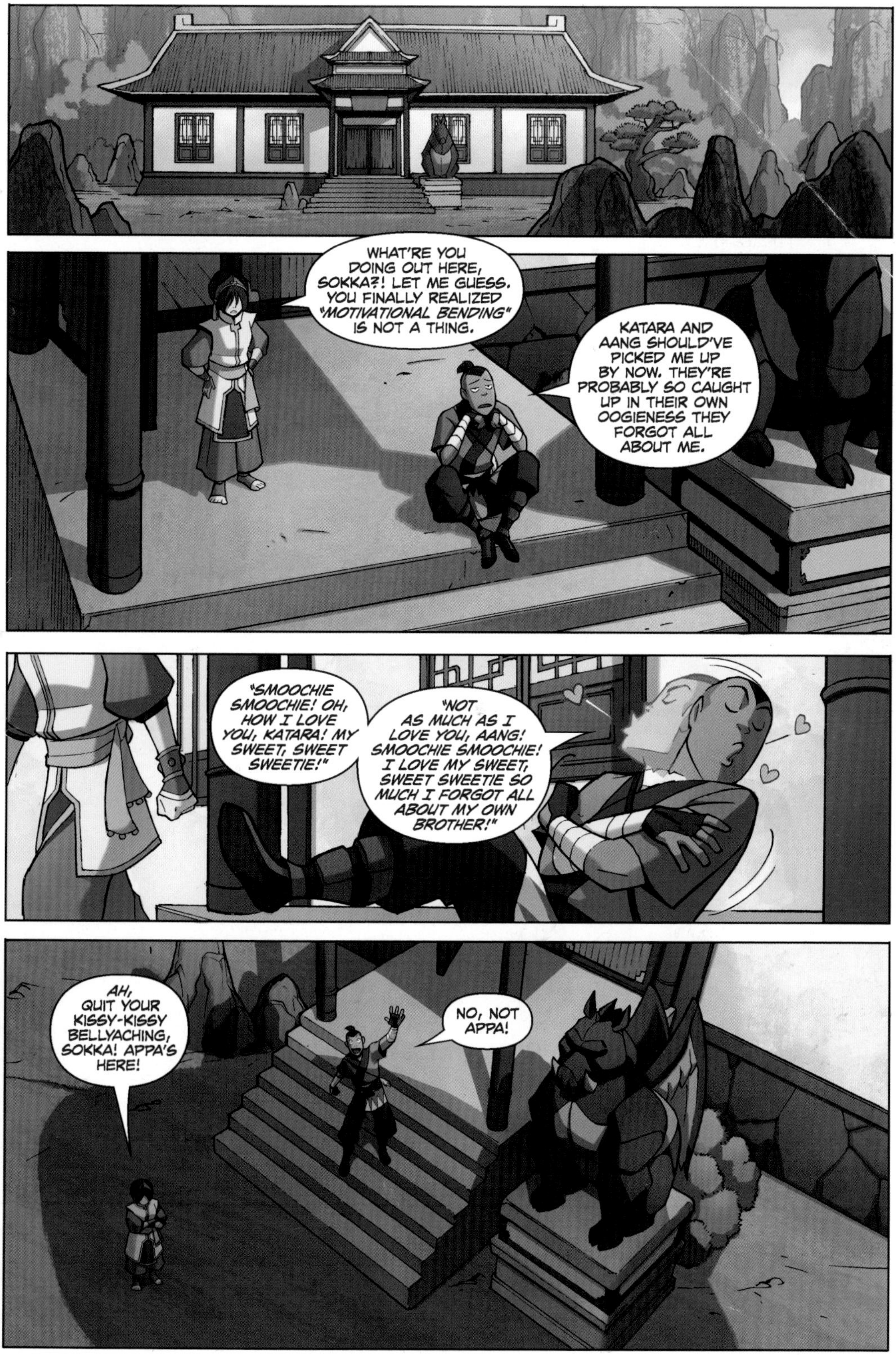
WHAT'RE YOU DOING OUT HERE, SOKKA?! LET ME GUESS. YOU FINALLY REALIZED "MOTIVATIONAL BENDING" IS NOT A THING.
KATARA AND AANG SHOULD'VE PICKED ME UP BY NOW. THEY'RE PROBABLY SO CAUGHT UP IN THEIR OWN OOGIENESS THEY FORGOT ALL ABOUT ME.
"SMOOCHIE SMOOCHIE! OH, HOW I LOVE YOU, KATARA! MY SWEET, SWEET SWEETIE!"
"NOT AS MUCH AS I LOVE YOU, AANG! SMOOCHIE SMOOCHIE! I LOVE MY SWEET, SWEET SWEETIE SO MUCH I FORGOT ALL ABOUT MY OWN BROTHER!"
AH, QUIT YOUR KISSY-KISSY BELLYACHING, SOKKA! APPA'S HERE!
NO, NOT APPA!

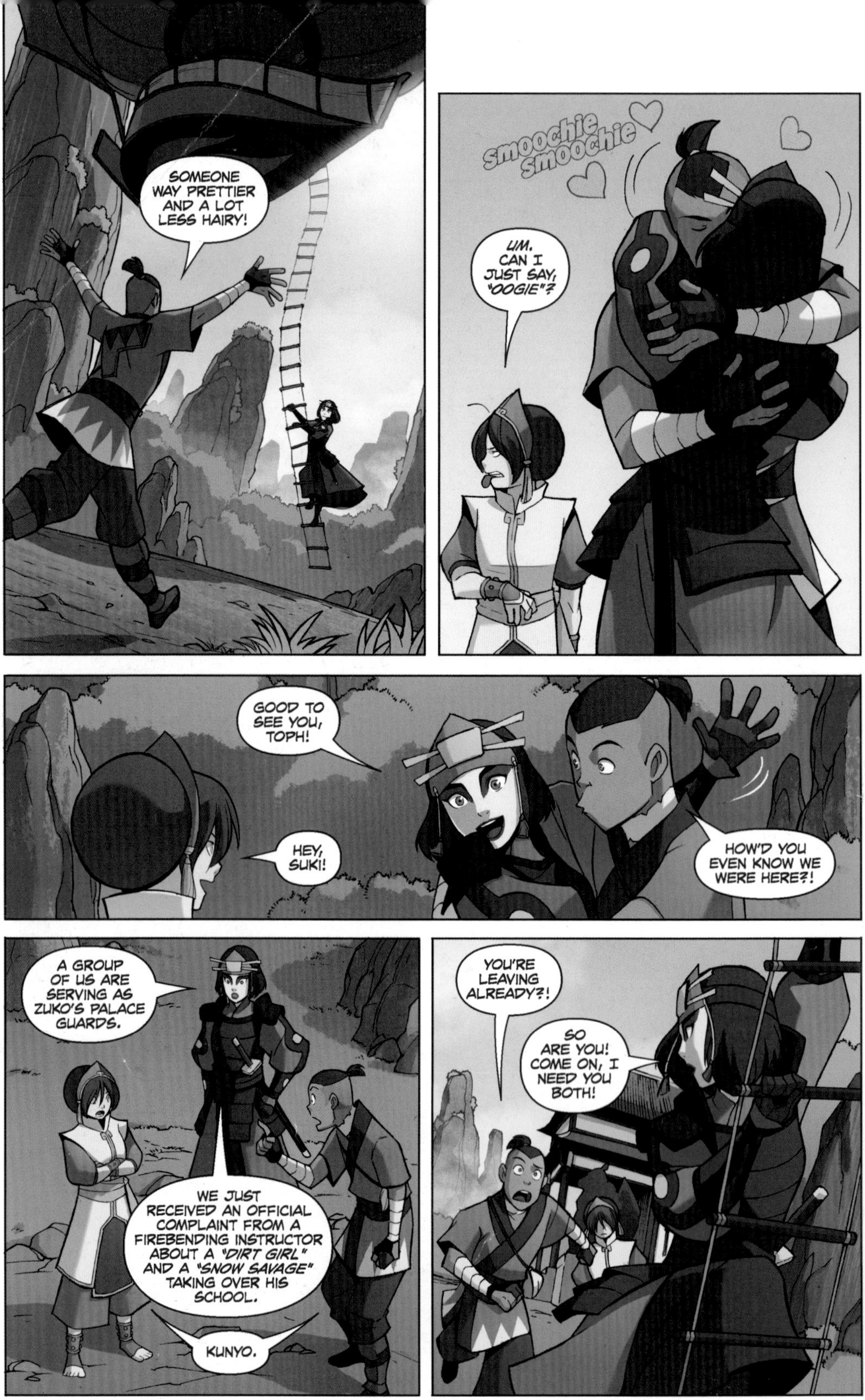
SOMEONE WAY PRETTIER AND A LOT LESS HAIRY!
smoochie smoochie
UM. CAN I JUST SAY, "OOGIE"?
GOOD TO SEE YOU, TOPH!
HEY, SUKI!
HOW'D YOU EVEN KNOW WE WERE HERE?!
A GROUP OF US ARE SERVING AS ZUKO'S PALACE GUARDS.
WE JUST RECEIVED AN OFFICIAL COMPLAINT FROM A FIREBENDING INSTRUCTOR ABOUT A "DIRT GIRL" AND A "SNOW SAVAGE" TAKING OVER HIS SCHOOL.
KUNYO.
YOU'RE LEAVING ALREADY?!
SO ARE YOU! COME ON, I NEED YOU BOTH!

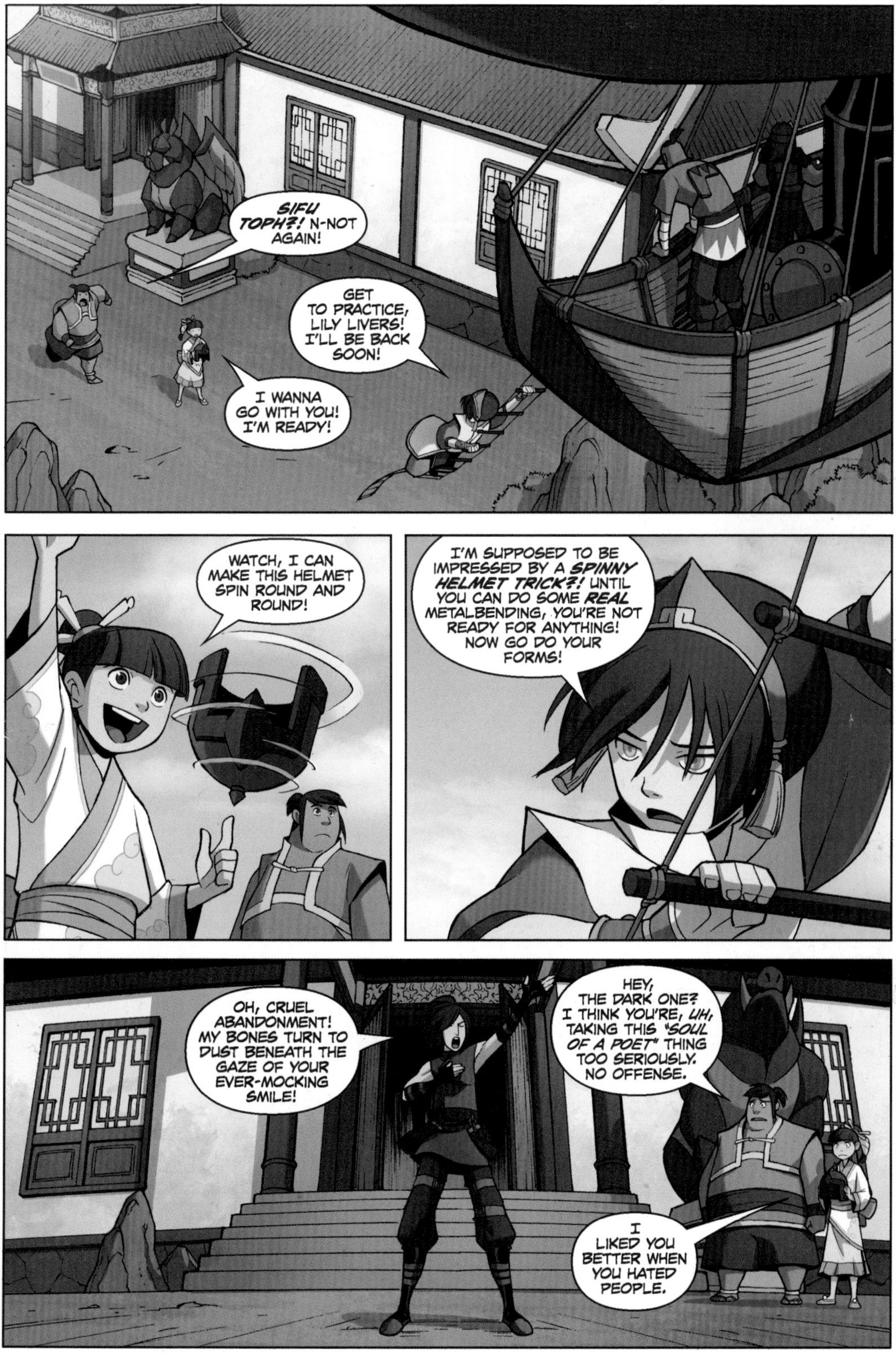
SIFU TOPH?! N-NOT AGAIN!
GET TO PRACTICE, LILY LIVERS! I'LL BE BACK SOON!
I WANNA GO WITH YOU! I'M READY!
WATCH, I CAN MAKE THIS HELMET SPIN ROUND AND ROUND!
I'M SUPPOSED TO BE IMPRESSED BY A SPINNY HELMET TRICK?! UNTIL YOU CAN DO SOME REAL METALBENDING, YOU'RE NOT READY FOR ANYTHING! NOW GO DO YOUR FORMS!
OH, CRUEL ABANDONMENT! MY BONES TURN TO DUST BENEATH THE GAZE OF YOUR EVER-MOCKING SMILE!
HEY, THE DARK ONE? I THINK YOU'RE, UH, TAKING THIS "SOUL OF A POET" THING TOO SERIOUSLY. NO OFFENSE.
I LIKED YOU BETTER WHEN YOU HATED PEOPLE.

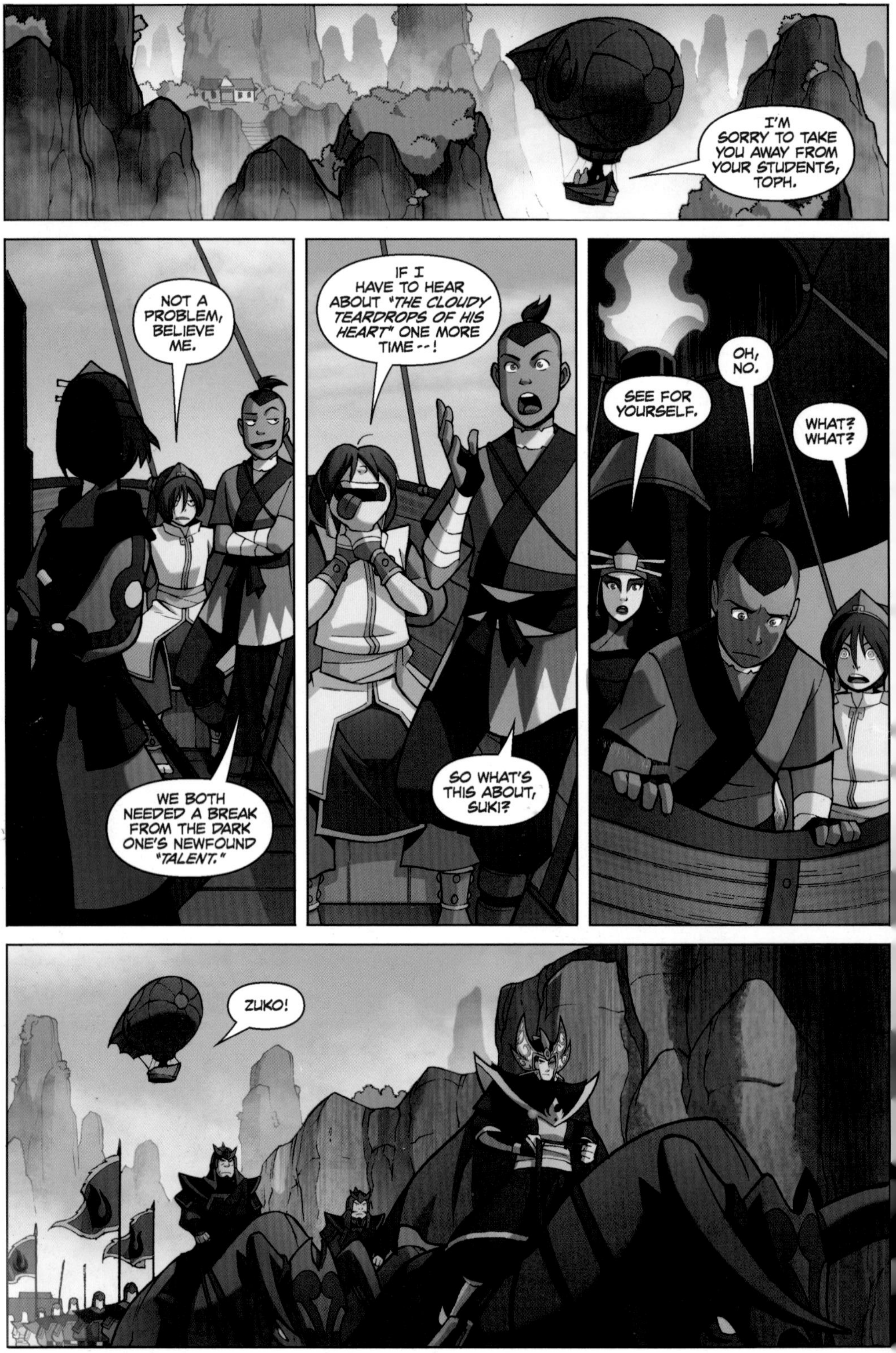
I'M SORRY TO TAKE YOU AWAY FROM YOUR STUDENTS, TOPH.
NOT A PROBLEM, BELIEVE ME.
WE BOTH NEEDED A BREAK FROM THE DARK ONE'S NEWFOUND "TALENT."
IF I HAVE TO HEAR ABOUT "THE CLOUDY TEARDROPS OF HIS HEART" ONE MORE TIME --!
SO WHAT'S THIS ABOUT, SUKI?
SEE FOR YOURSELF.
OH, NO.
WHAT? WHAT?
ZUKO!

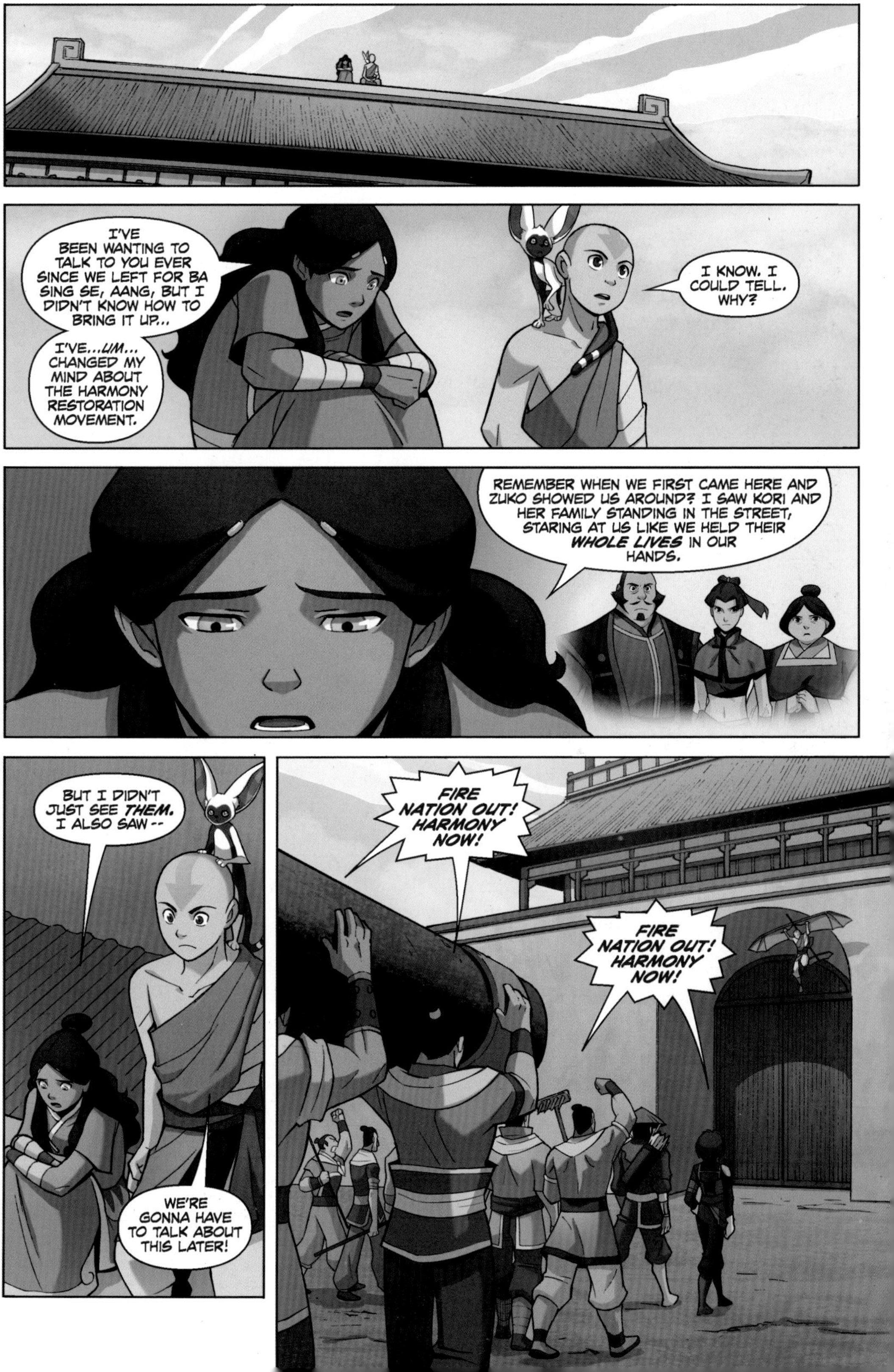
I'VE BEEN WANTING TO TALK TO YOU EVER SINCE WE LEFT FOR BA SING SE, AANG, BUT I DIDN'T KNOW HOW TO BRING IT UP...
I'VE...*UM*... CHANGED MY MIND ABOUT THE HARMONY RESTORATION MOVEMENT.
I KNOW. I COULD TELL. WHY?
REMEMBER WHEN WE FIRST CAME HERE AND ZUKO SHOWED US AROUND? I SAW KORI AND HER FAMILY STANDING IN THE STREET, STARING AT US LIKE WE HELD THEIR *WHOLE LIVES* IN OUR HANDS.
BUT I DIDN'T JUST SEE *THEM*. I ALSO SAW --
FIRE NATION OUT! HARMONY NOW!
FIRE NATION OUT! HARMONY NOW!
WE'RE GONNA HAVE TO TALK ABOUT THIS LATER!

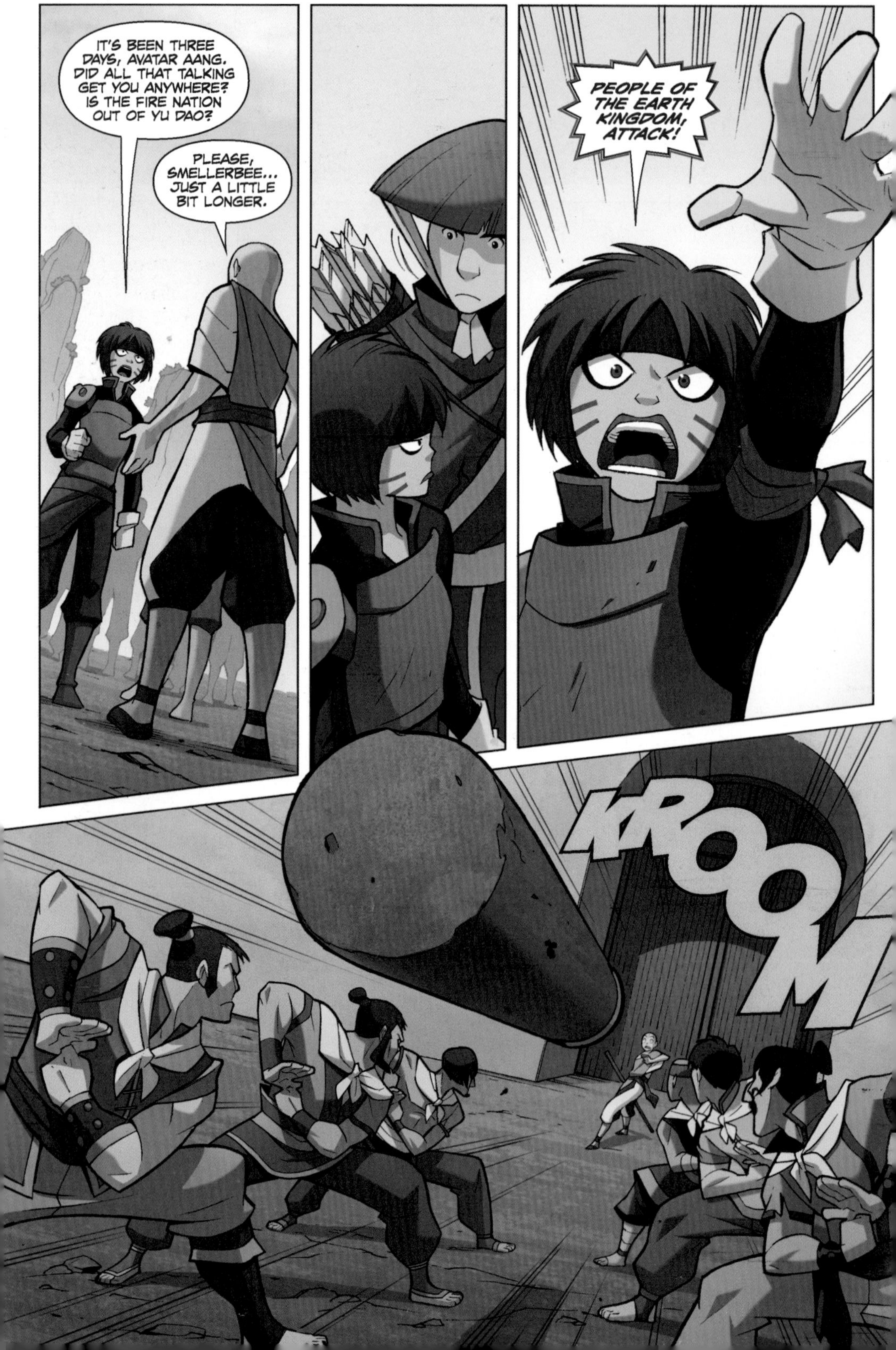
IT'S BEEN THREE DAYS, AVATAR AANG. DID ALL THAT TALKING GET YOU ANYWHERE? IS THE FIRE NATION OUT OF YU DAO?
PLEASE, SMELLERBEE... JUST A LITTLE BIT LONGER.
PEOPLE OF THE EARTH KINGDOM, ATTACK!
KROOM

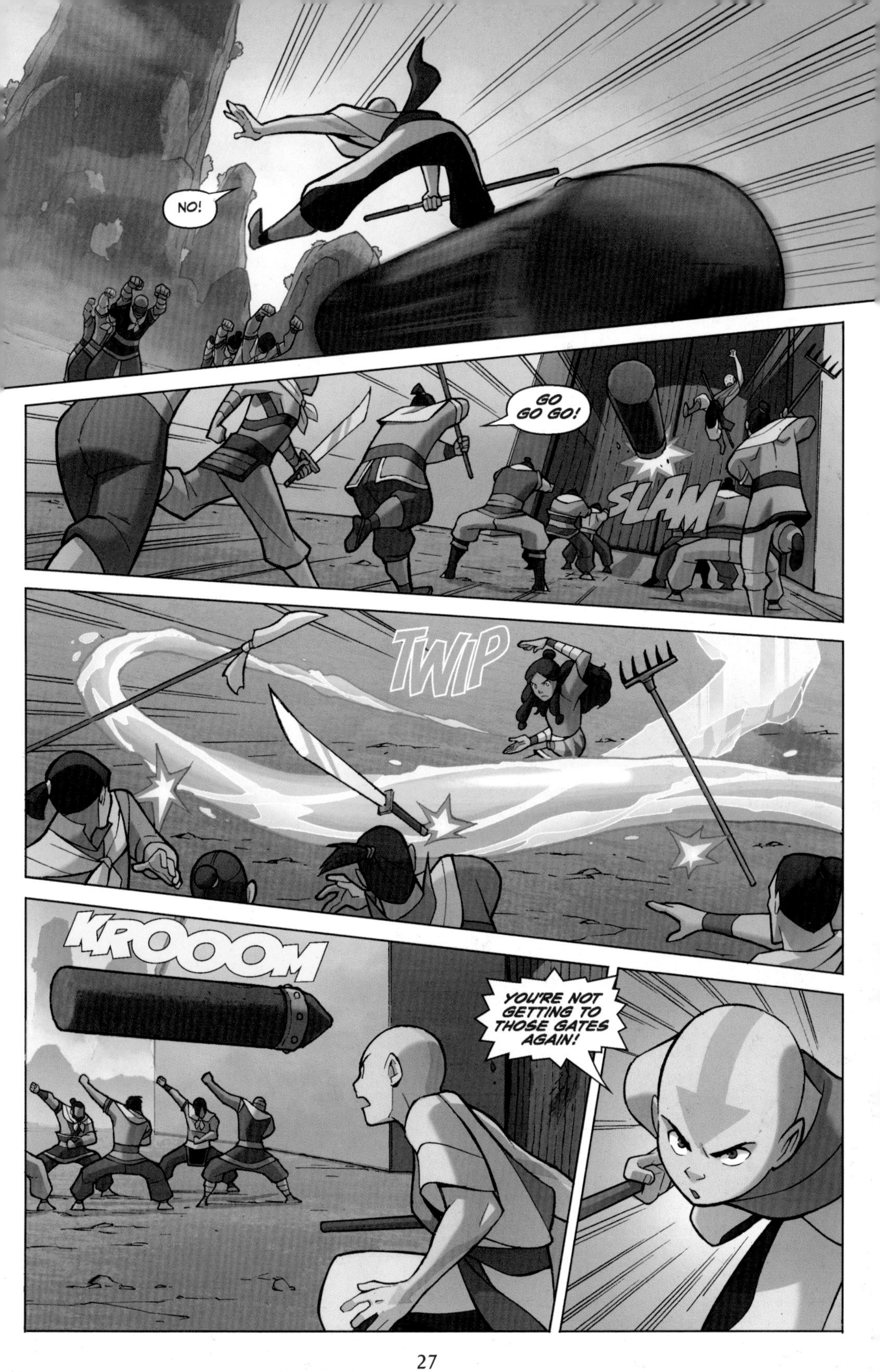
NO!
GO GO GO!
SLAM
TWIP
KROOOM
YOU'RE NOT GETTING TO THOSE GATES AGAIN!

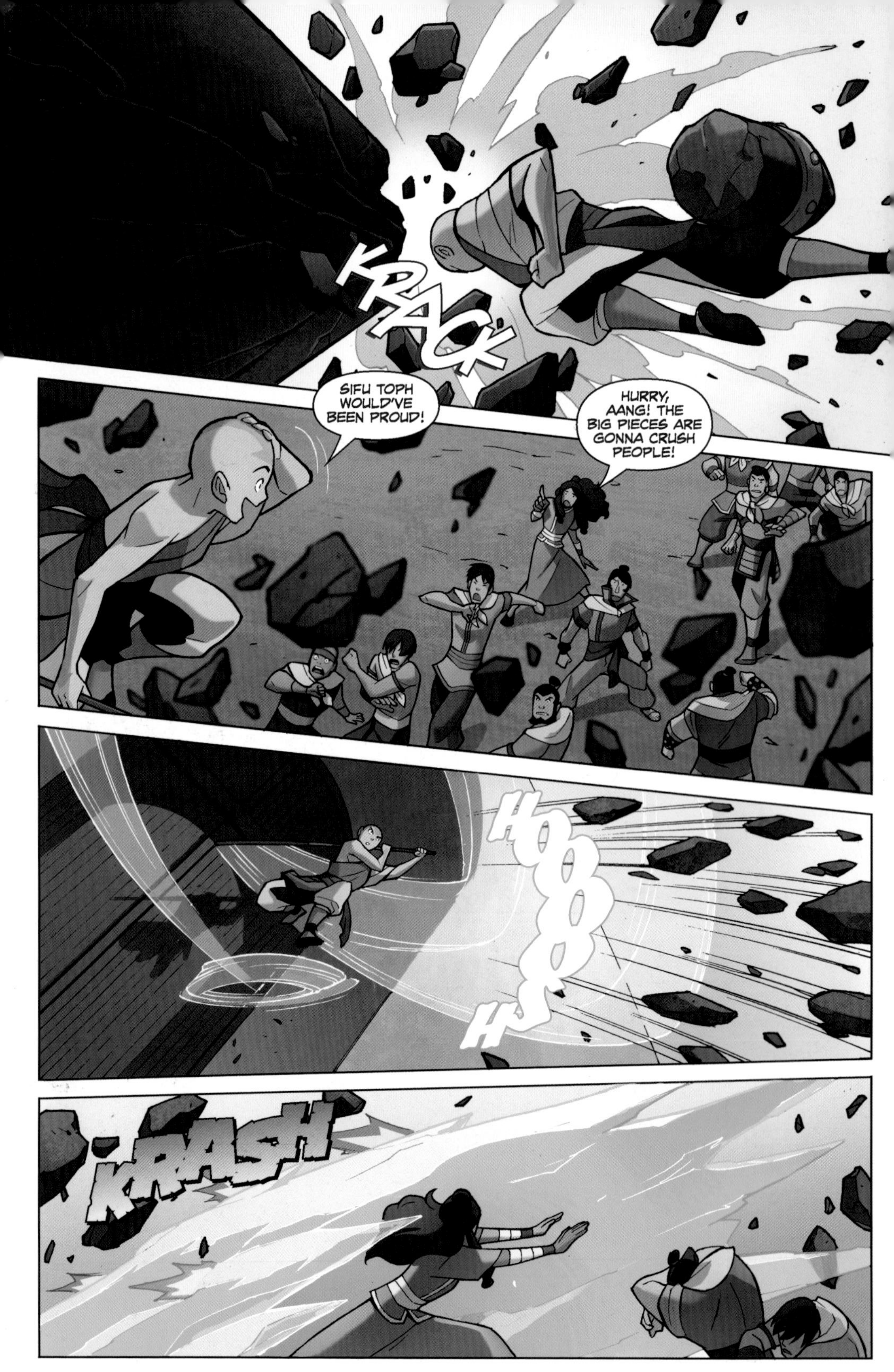
KRACK
SIFU TOPH WOULD'VE BEEN PROUD!
HURRY, AANG! THE BIG PIECES ARE GONNA CRUSH PEOPLE!
HOOSH
KRASH

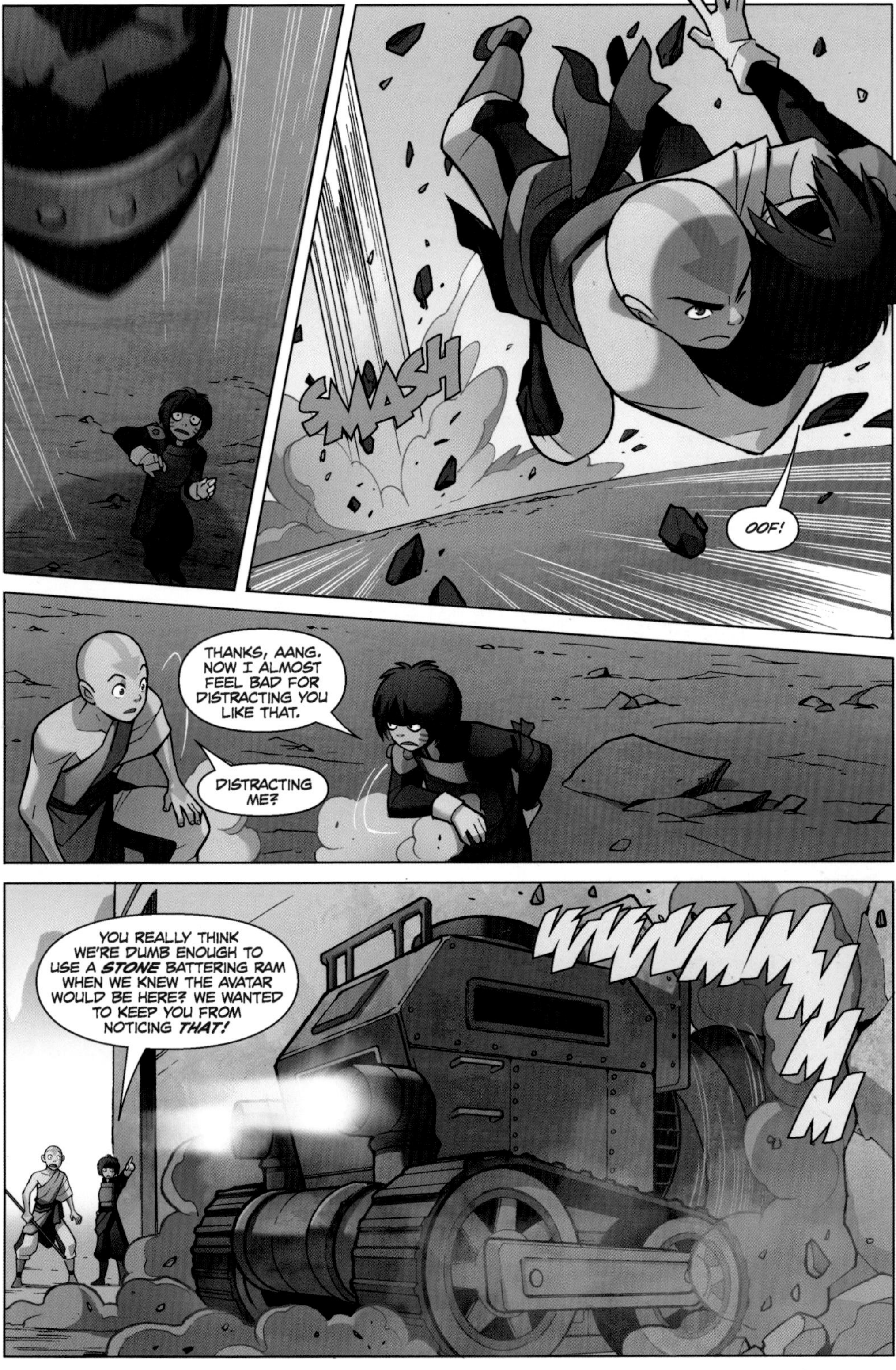
SMASH
OOF!
THANKS, AANG. NOW I ALMOST FEEL BAD FOR DISTRACTING YOU LIKE THAT.
DISTRACTING ME?
YOU REALLY THINK WE'RE DUMB ENOUGH TO USE A STONE BATTERING RAM WHEN WE KNEW THE AVATAR WOULD BE HERE? WE WANTED TO KEEP YOU FROM NOTICING THAT!
WWWWMMMMMM

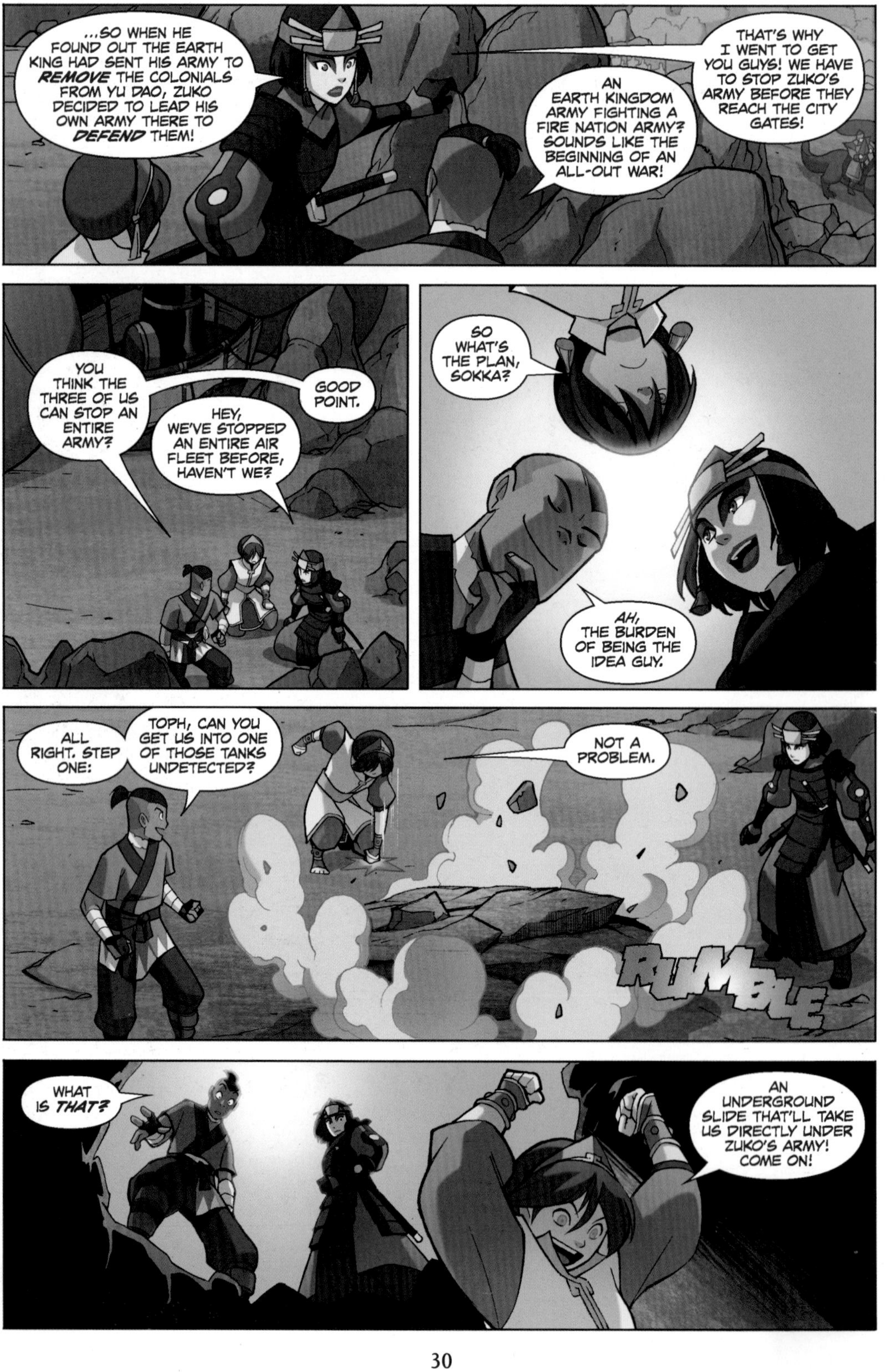
...SO WHEN HE FOUND OUT THE EARTH KING HAD SENT HIS ARMY TO *REMOVE* THE COLONIALS FROM YU DAO, ZUKO DECIDED TO LEAD HIS OWN ARMY THERE TO *DEFEND* THEM!
AN EARTH KINGDOM ARMY FIGHTING A FIRE NATION ARMY? SOUNDS LIKE THE BEGINNING OF AN ALL-OUT WAR!
THAT'S WHY I WENT TO GET YOU GUYS! WE HAVE TO STOP ZUKO'S ARMY BEFORE THEY REACH THE CITY GATES!
YOU THINK THE THREE OF US CAN STOP AN ENTIRE ARMY?
HEY, WE'VE STOPPED AN ENTIRE AIR FLEET BEFORE, HAVEN'T WE?
GOOD POINT.
SO WHAT'S THE PLAN, SOKKA?
AH, THE BURDEN OF BEING THE IDEA GUY.
ALL RIGHT. STEP ONE:
TOPH, CAN YOU GET US INTO ONE OF THOSE TANKS UNDETECTED?
NOT A PROBLEM.
RUMBLE
WHAT IS *THAT?*
AN UNDERGROUND SLIDE THAT'LL TAKE US DIRECTLY UNDER ZUKO'S ARMY! COME ON!

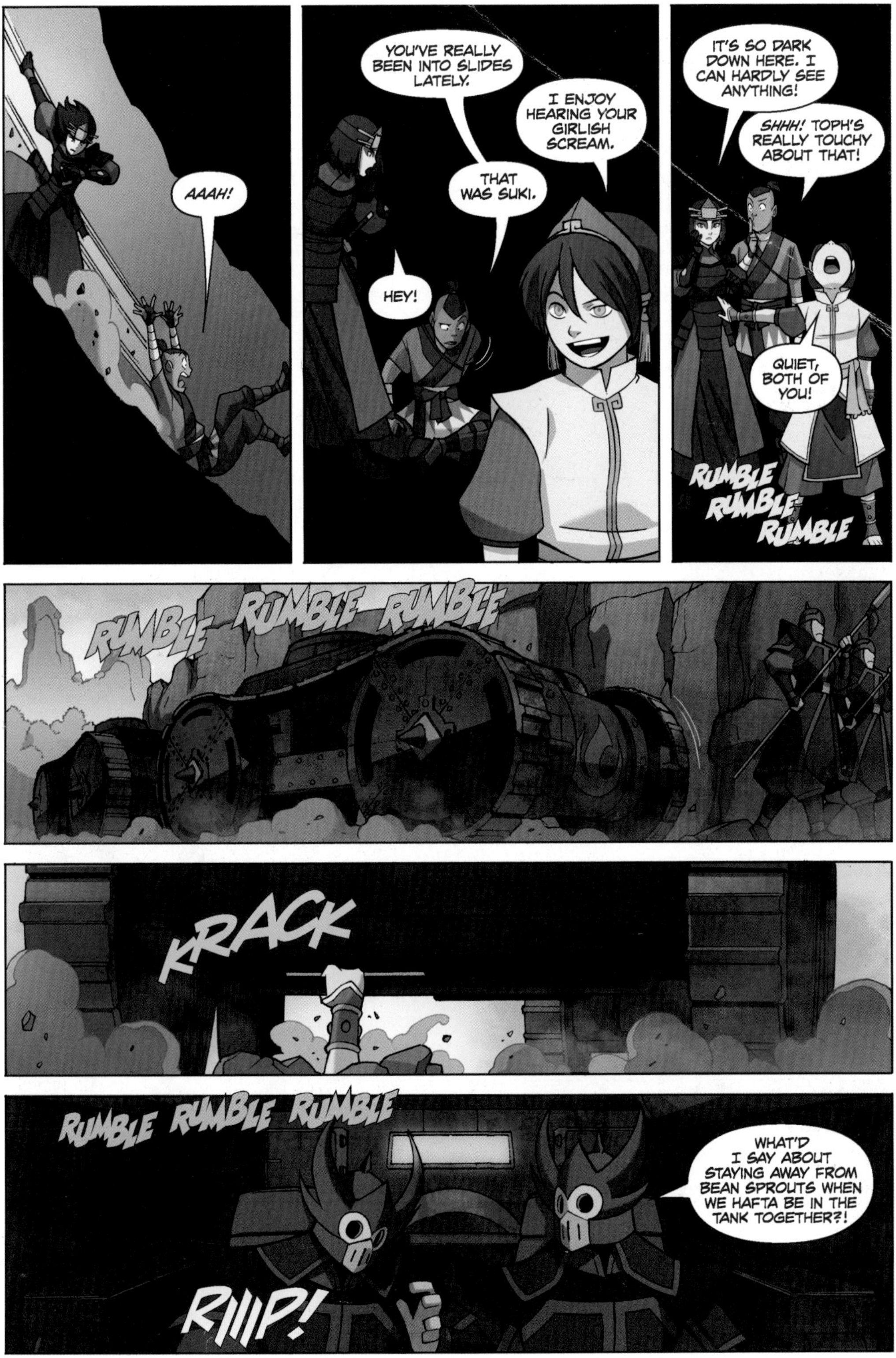
AAAH!
YOU'VE REALLY BEEN INTO SLIDES LATELY.
THAT WAS SUKI.
HEY!
I ENJOY HEARING YOUR GIRLISH SCREAM.
IT'S SO DARK DOWN HERE. I CAN HARDLY SEE ANYTHING!
SHHH! TOPH'S REALLY TOUCHY ABOUT THAT!
QUIET, BOTH OF YOU!
RUMBLE RUMBLE RUMBLE
RUMBLE RUMBLE RUMBLE
KRACK
RUMBLE RUMBLE RUMBLE
WHAT'D I SAY ABOUT STAYING AWAY FROM BEAN SPROUTS WHEN WE HAFTA BE IN THE TANK TOGETHER?!
RIIIP!

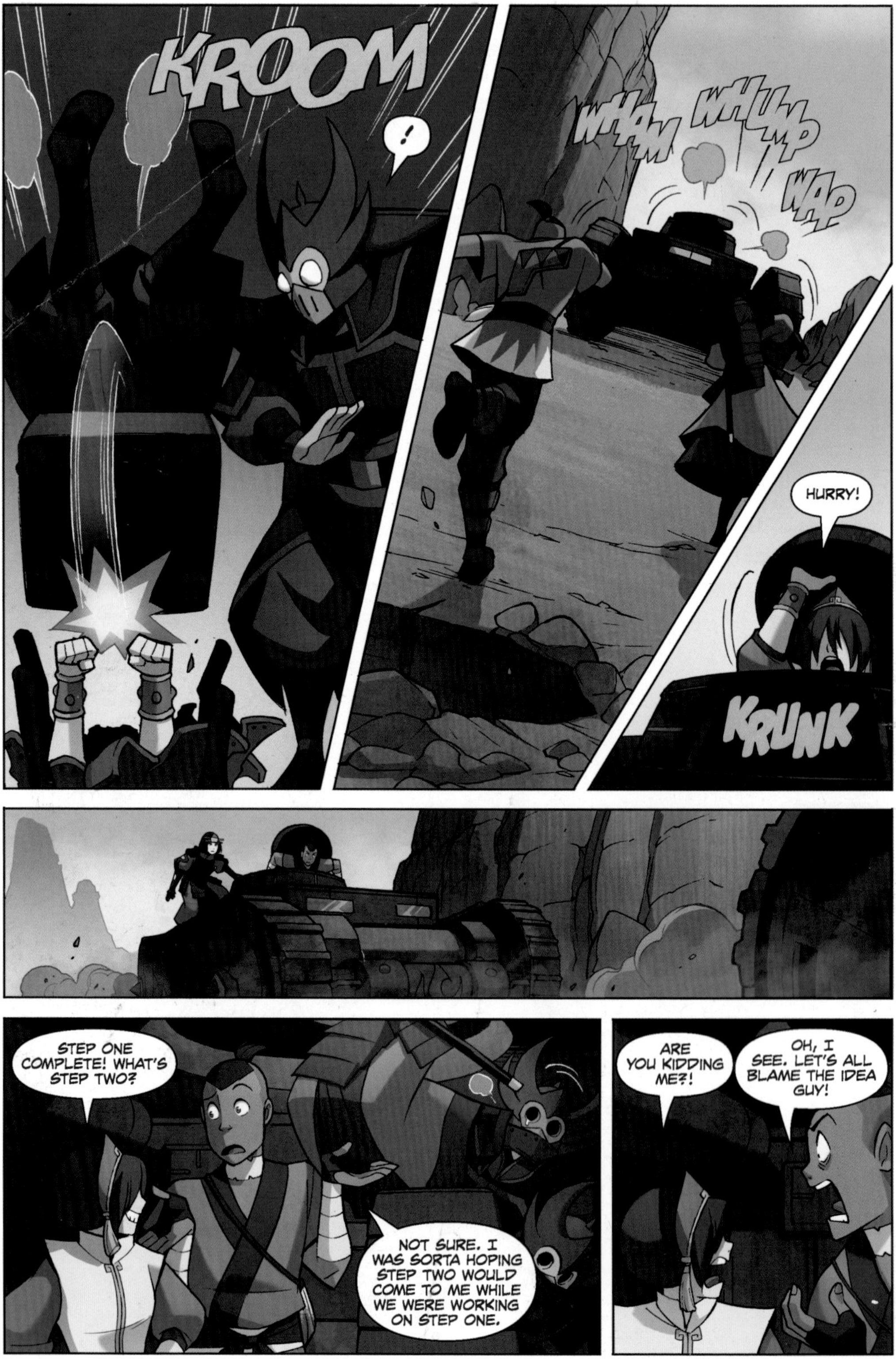
KROOM
!
WHAM
WHUMP
WAP
HURRY!
KRUNK
STEP ONE COMPLETE! WHAT'S STEP TWO?
NOT SURE. I WAS SORTA HOPING STEP TWO WOULD COME TO ME WHILE WE WERE WORKING ON STEP ONE.
ARE YOU KIDDING ME?!
OH, I SEE. LET'S ALL BLAME THE IDEA GUY!

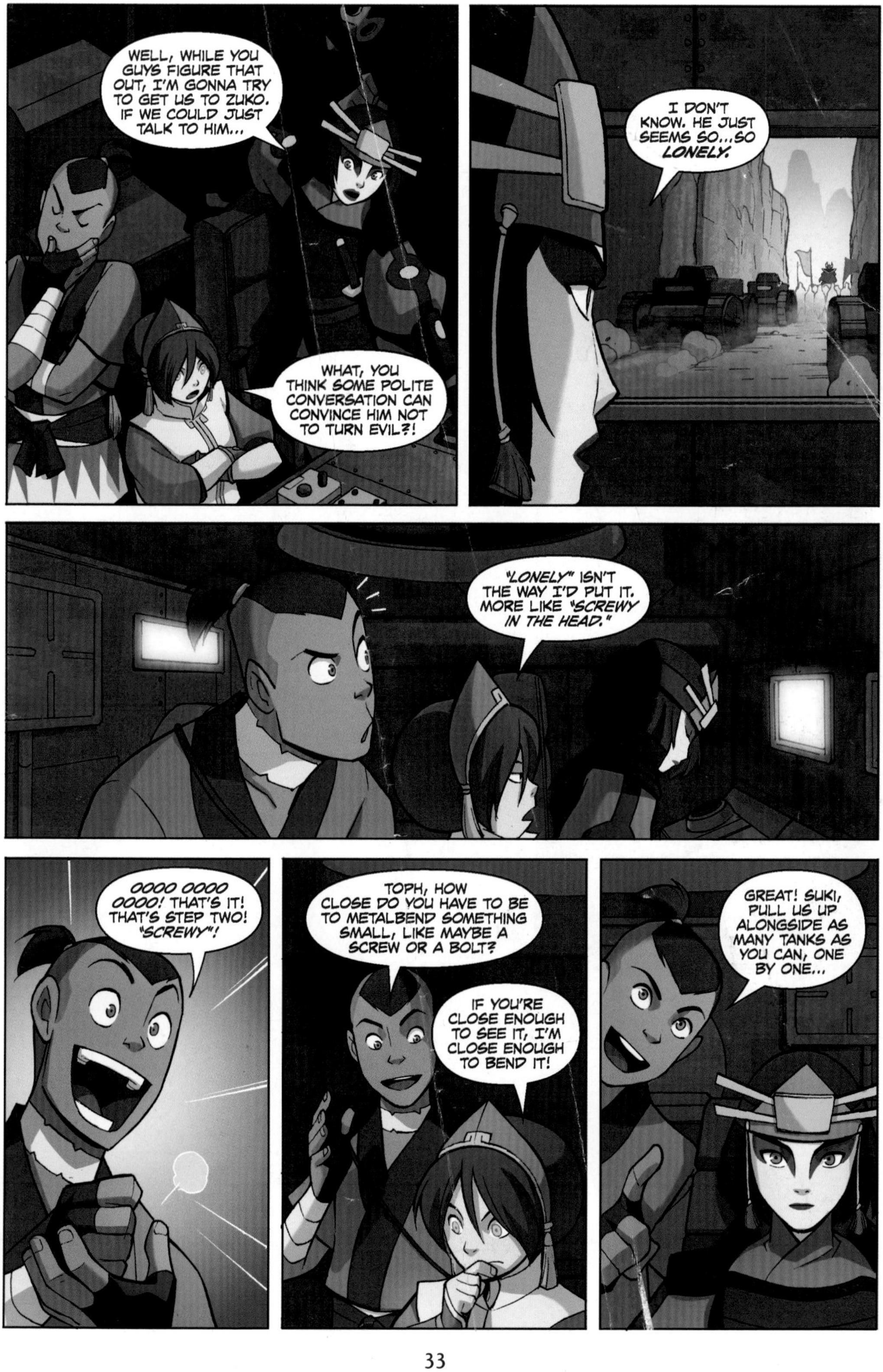
WELL, WHILE YOU GUYS FIGURE THAT OUT, I'M GONNA TRY TO GET US TO ZUKO. IF WE COULD JUST TALK TO HIM...
WHAT, YOU THINK SOME POLITE CONVERSATION CAN CONVINCE HIM NOT TO TURN EVIL?!
I DON'T KNOW. HE JUST SEEMS SO...SO *LONELY.*
"LONELY" ISN'T THE WAY I'D PUT IT. MORE LIKE *"SCREWY IN THE HEAD."*
OOOO OOOO OOOO! THAT'S IT! THAT'S STEP TWO! *"SCREWY"*!
TOPH, HOW CLOSE DO YOU HAVE TO BE TO METALBEND SOMETHING SMALL, LIKE MAYBE A SCREW OR A BOLT?
IF YOU'RE CLOSE ENOUGH TO SEE IT, I'M CLOSE ENOUGH TO BEND IT!
GREAT! SUKI, PULL US UP ALONGSIDE AS MANY TANKS AS YOU CAN, ONE BY ONE...

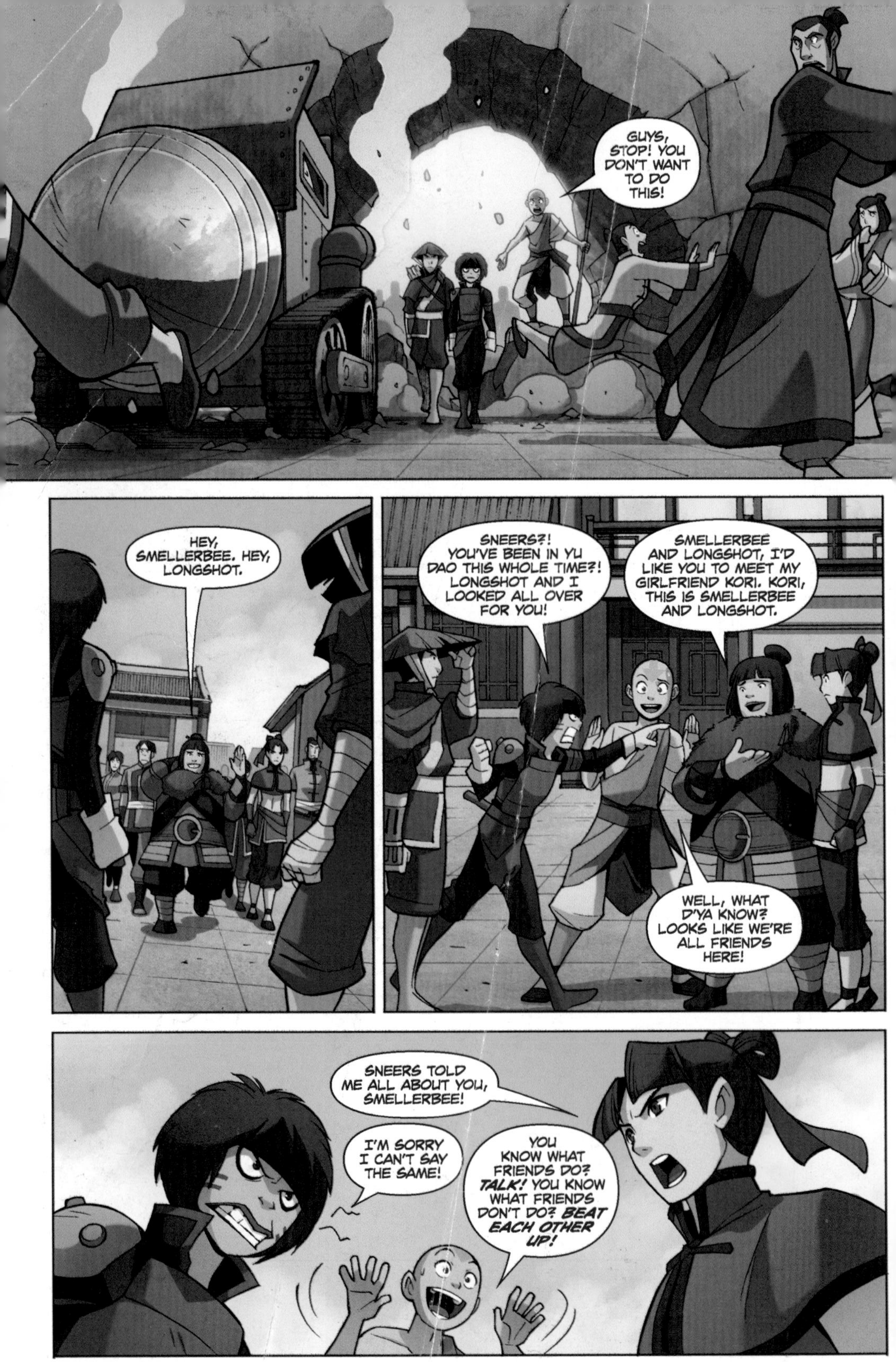
GUYS, STOP! YOU DON'T WANT TO DO THIS!
HEY, SMELLERBEE. HEY, LONGSHOT.
SNEERS?! YOU'VE BEEN IN YU DAO THIS WHOLE TIME?! LONGSHOT AND I LOOKED ALL OVER FOR YOU!
SMELLERBEE AND LONGSHOT, I'D LIKE YOU TO MEET MY GIRLFRIEND KORI. KORI, THIS IS SMELLERBEE AND LONGSHOT.
WELL, WHAT D'YA KNOW? LOOKS LIKE WE'RE ALL FRIENDS HERE!
SNEERS TOLD ME ALL ABOUT YOU, SMELLERBEE!
I'M SORRY I CAN'T SAY THE SAME!
YOU KNOW WHAT FRIENDS DO? *TALK!* YOU KNOW WHAT FRIENDS DON'T DO? *BEAT EACH OTHER UP!*

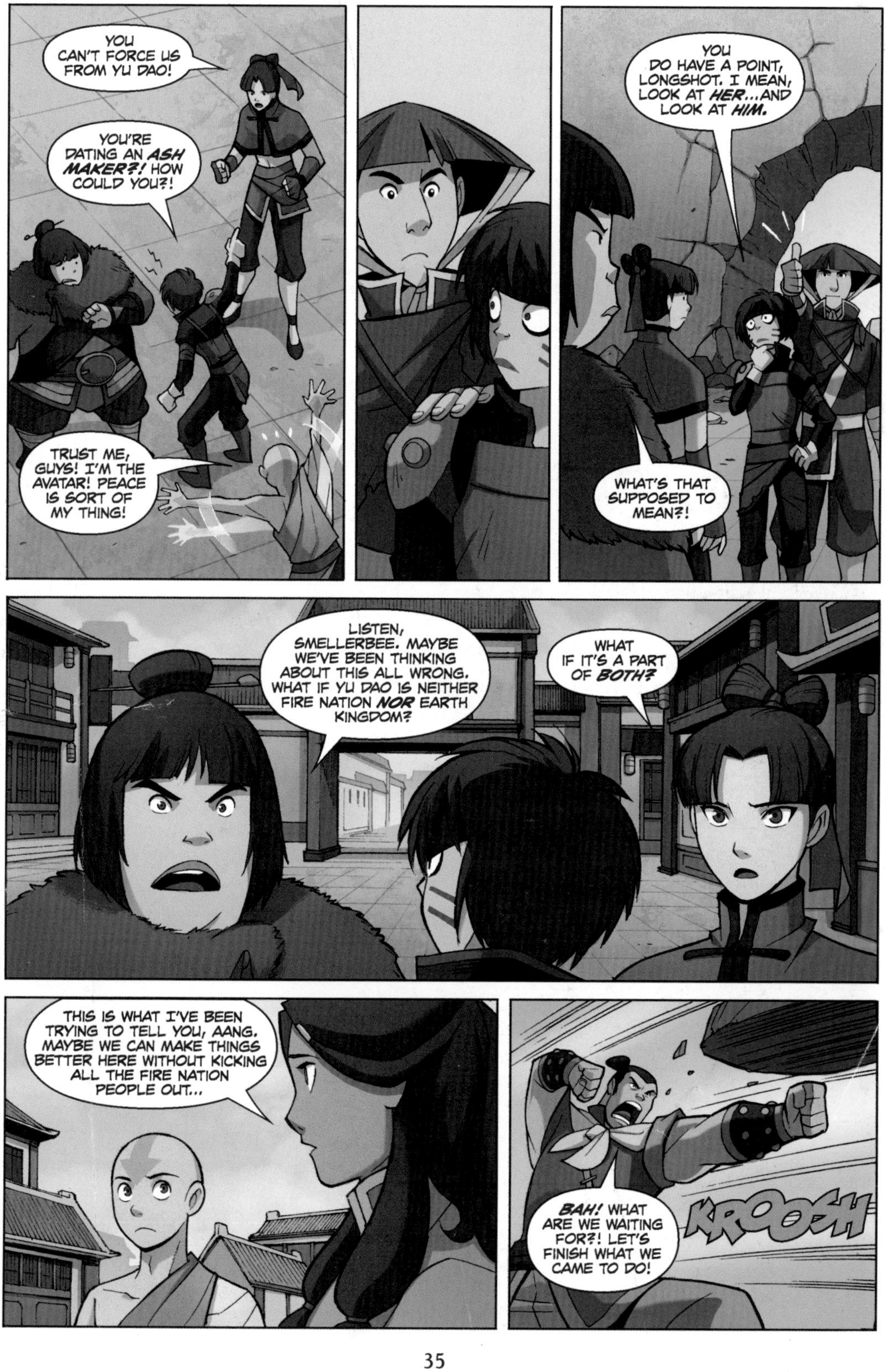
YOU CAN'T FORCE US FROM YU DAO!
YOU'RE DATING AN ASH MAKER?! HOW COULD YOU?!
TRUST ME, GUYS! I'M THE AVATAR! PEACE IS SORT OF MY THING!
YOU DO HAVE A POINT, LONGSHOT. I MEAN, LOOK AT HER...AND LOOK AT HIM.
WHAT'S THAT SUPPOSED TO MEAN?!
LISTEN, SMELLERBEE. MAYBE WE'VE BEEN THINKING ABOUT THIS ALL WRONG. WHAT IF YU DAO IS NEITHER FIRE NATION NOR EARTH KINGDOM?
WHAT IF IT'S A PART OF BOTH?
THIS IS WHAT I'VE BEEN TRYING TO TELL YOU, AANG. MAYBE WE CAN MAKE THINGS BETTER HERE WITHOUT KICKING ALL THE FIRE NATION PEOPLE OUT...
BAH! WHAT ARE WE WAITING FOR?! LET'S FINISH WHAT WE CAME TO DO!
KROOSH

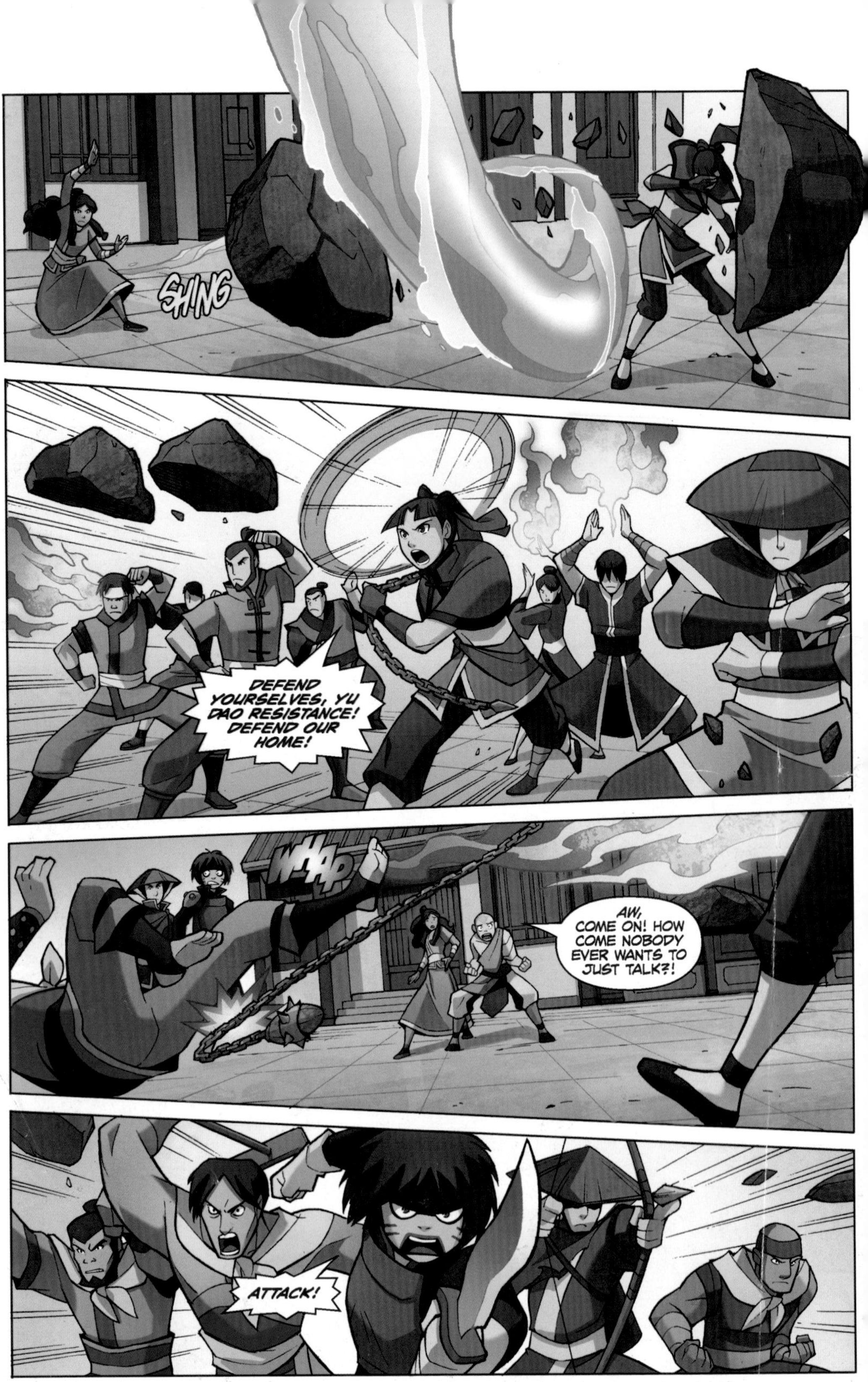
SHING
DEFEND YOURSELVES, YU DAO RESISTANCE! DEFEND OUR HOME!
WHAP
AW, COME ON! HOW COME NOBODY EVER WANTS TO JUST TALK?!
ATTACK!

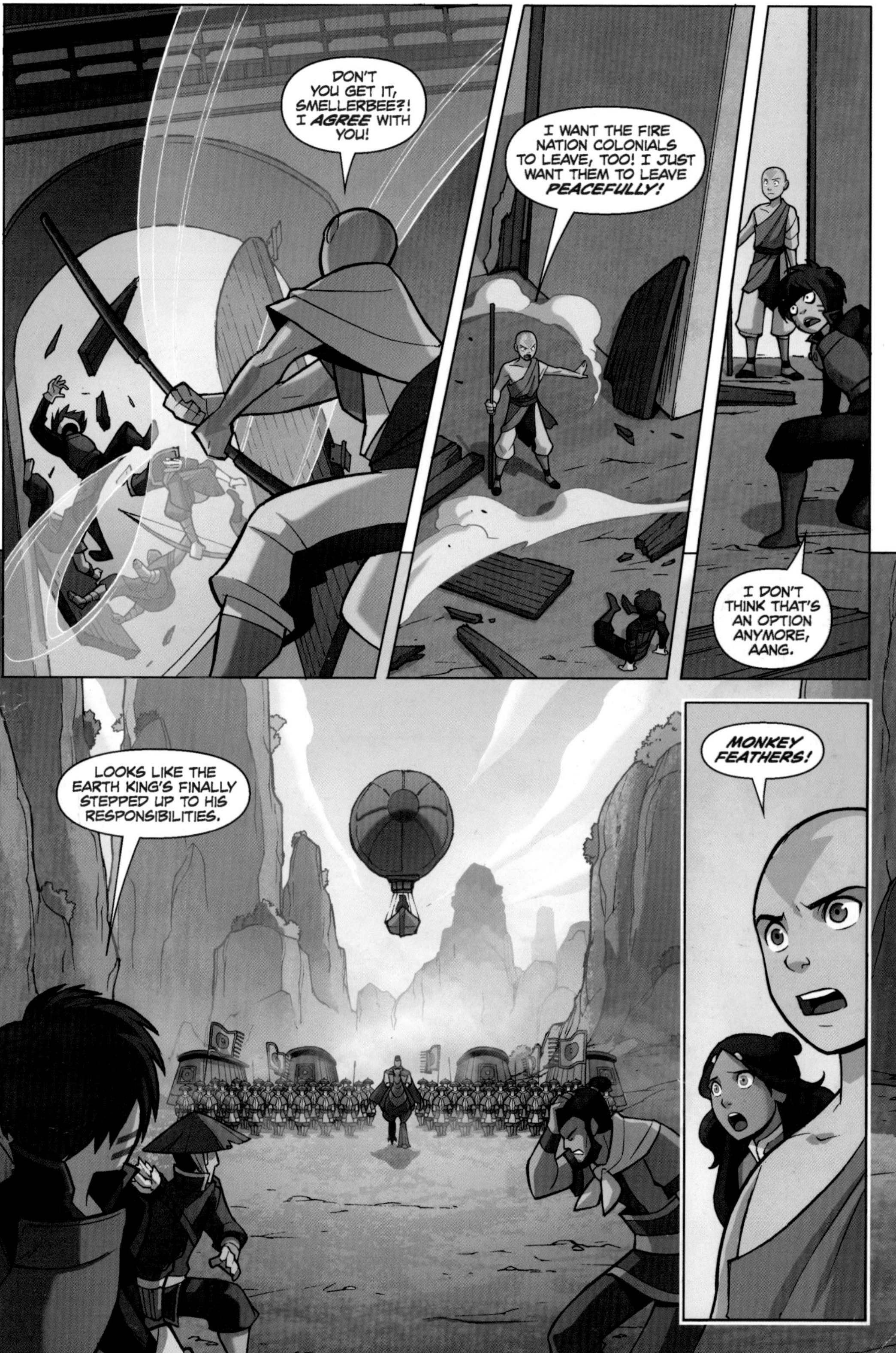
DON'T YOU GET IT, SMELLERBEE?! I AGREE WITH YOU!
I WANT THE FIRE NATION COLONIALS TO LEAVE, TOO! I JUST WANT THEM TO LEAVE PEACEFULLY!
I DON'T THINK THAT'S AN OPTION ANYMORE, AANG.
LOOKS LIKE THE EARTH KING'S FINALLY STEPPED UP TO HIS RESPONSIBILITIES.
MONKEY FEATHERS!

AVATAR AANG!

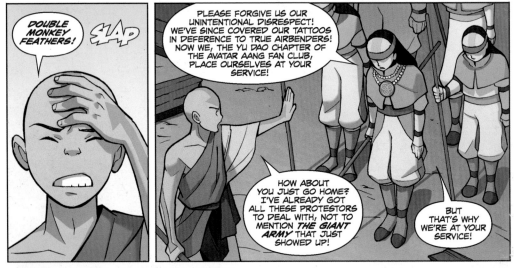

DOUBLE MONKEY FEATHERS! *SLAP*

PLEASE FORGIVE US OUR UNINTENTIONAL DISRESPECT! WE'VE SINCE COVERED OUR TATTOOS IN DEFERENCE TO TRUE AIRBENDERS! NOW WE, THE YU DAO CHAPTER OF THE AVATAR AANG FAN CLUB, PLACE OURSELVES AT YOUR SERVICE!

HOW ABOUT YOU JUST GO HOME? I'VE ALREADY GOT ALL THESE PROTESTORS TO DEAL WITH, NOT TO MENTION *THE GIANT ARMY* THAT JUST SHOWED UP!

BUT THAT'S WHY WE'RE AT YOUR SERVICE!

KRUNCH

ATTENTION, ATTENTION! BY OFFICIAL DECREE OF EARTH KING KUEI, THE EARTH KINGDOM *RECLAIMS* THE FORMER FIRE NATION COLONY OF YU DAO!

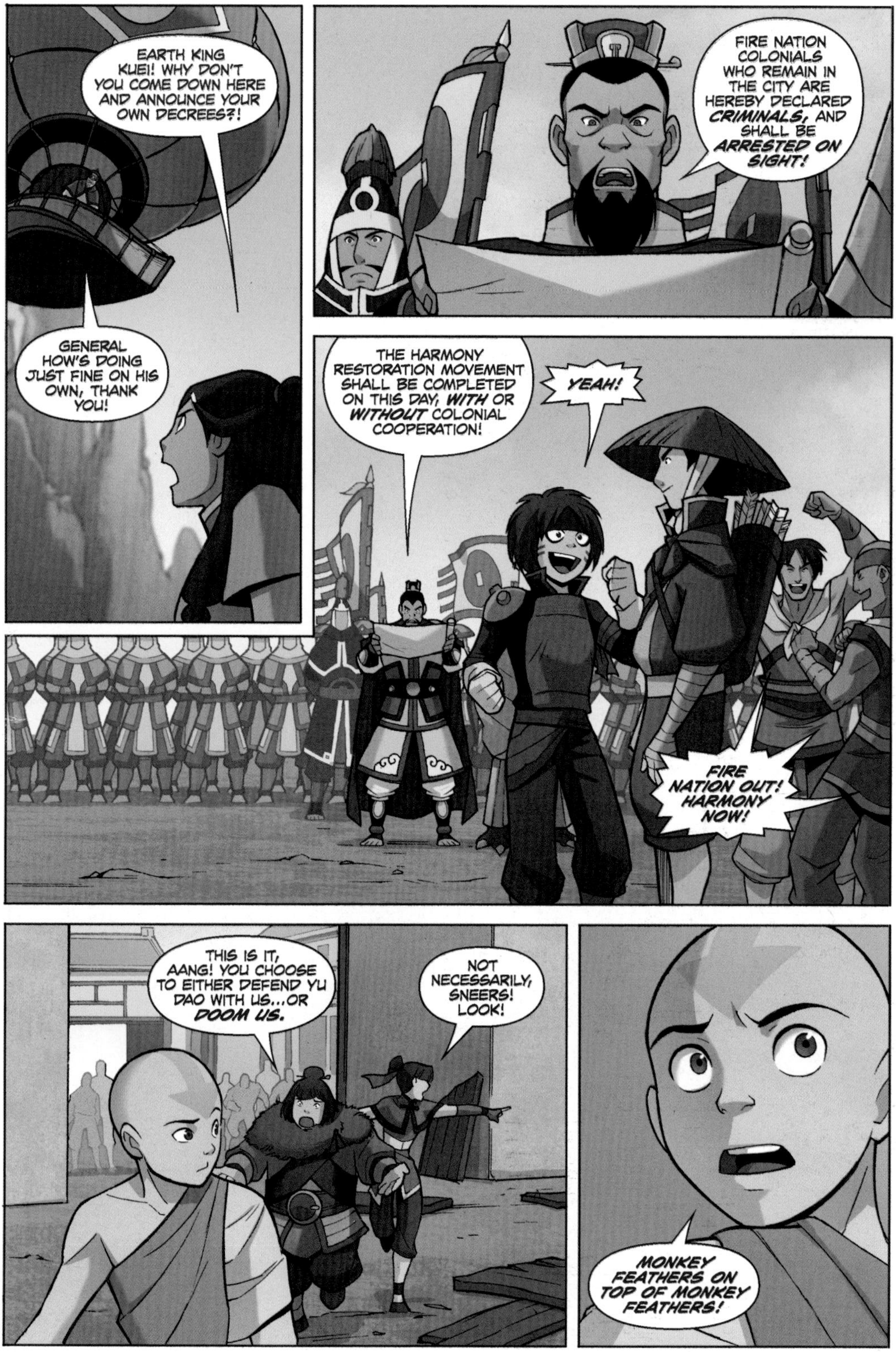
EARTH KING KUEI! WHY DON'T YOU COME DOWN HERE AND ANNOUNCE YOUR OWN DECREES?!
GENERAL HOW'S DOING JUST FINE ON HIS OWN, THANK YOU!
FIRE NATION COLONIALS WHO REMAIN IN THE CITY ARE HEREBY DECLARED CRIMINALS, AND SHALL BE ARRESTED ON SIGHT!
THE HARMONY RESTORATION MOVEMENT SHALL BE COMPLETED ON THIS DAY, WITH OR WITHOUT COLONIAL COOPERATION!
YEAH!
FIRE NATION OUT! HARMONY NOW!
THIS IS IT, AANG! YOU CHOOSE TO EITHER DEFEND YU DAO WITH US...OR DOOM US.
NOT NECESSARILY, SNEERS! LOOK!
MONKEY FEATHERS ON TOP OF MONKEY FEATHERS!

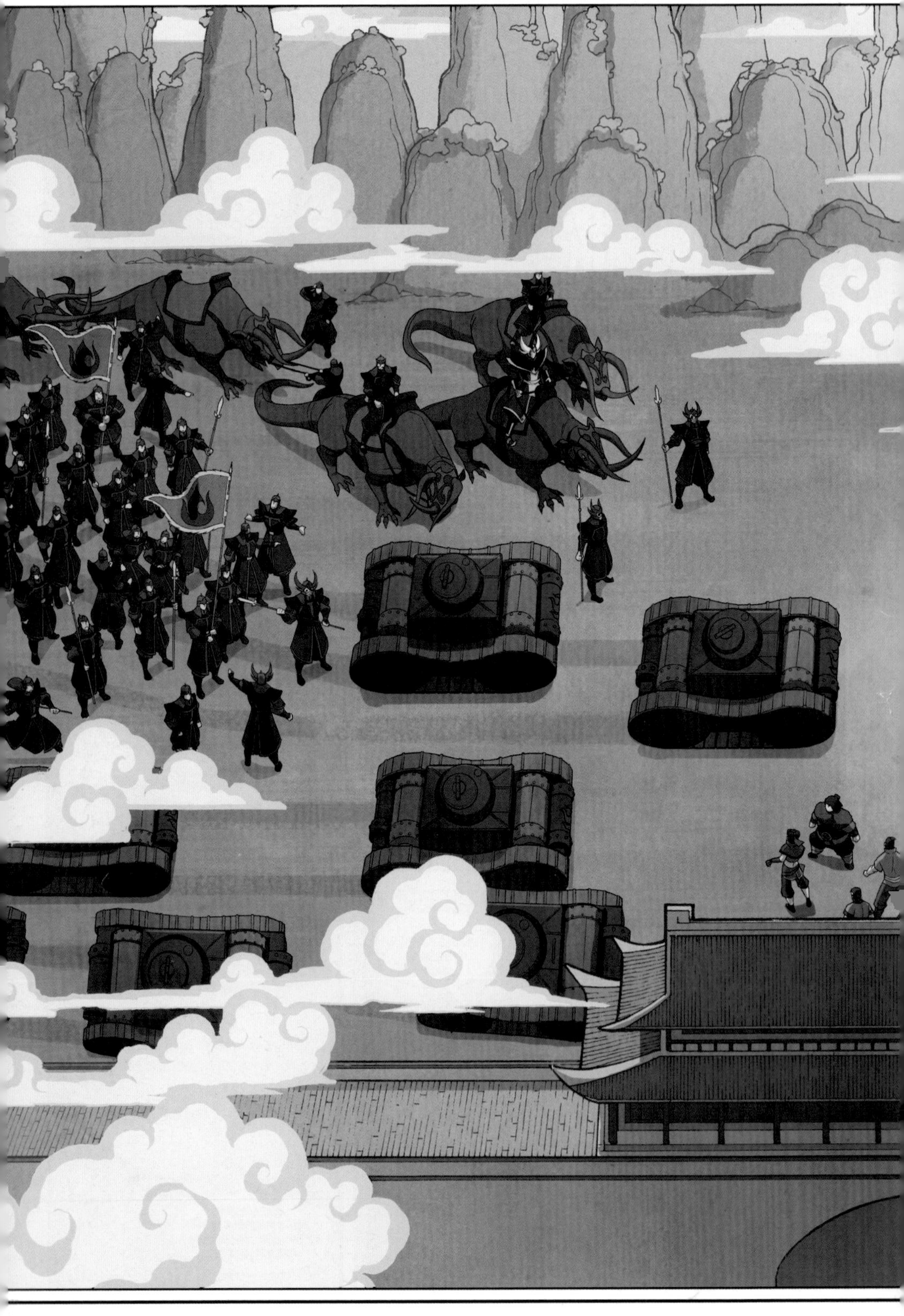

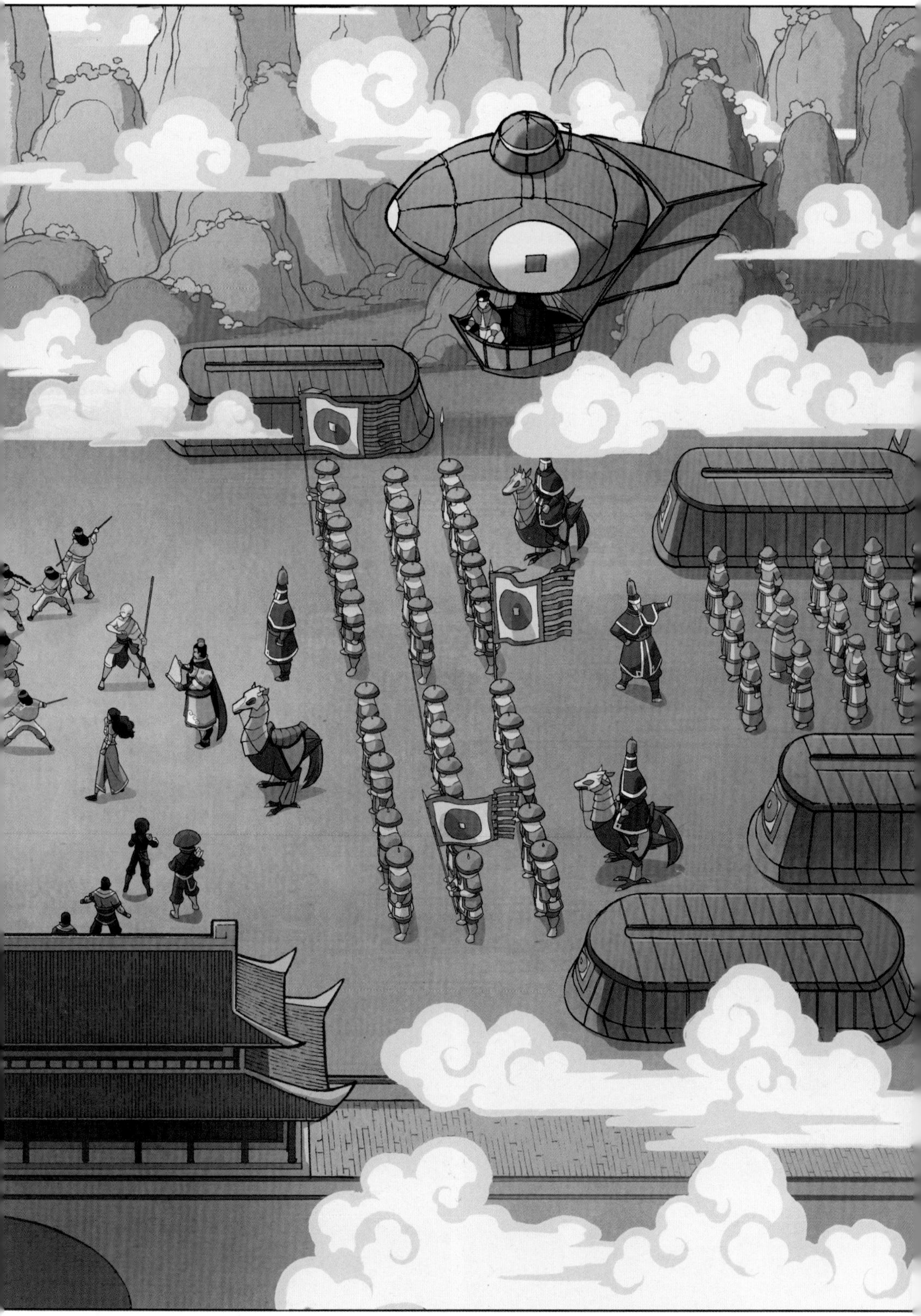

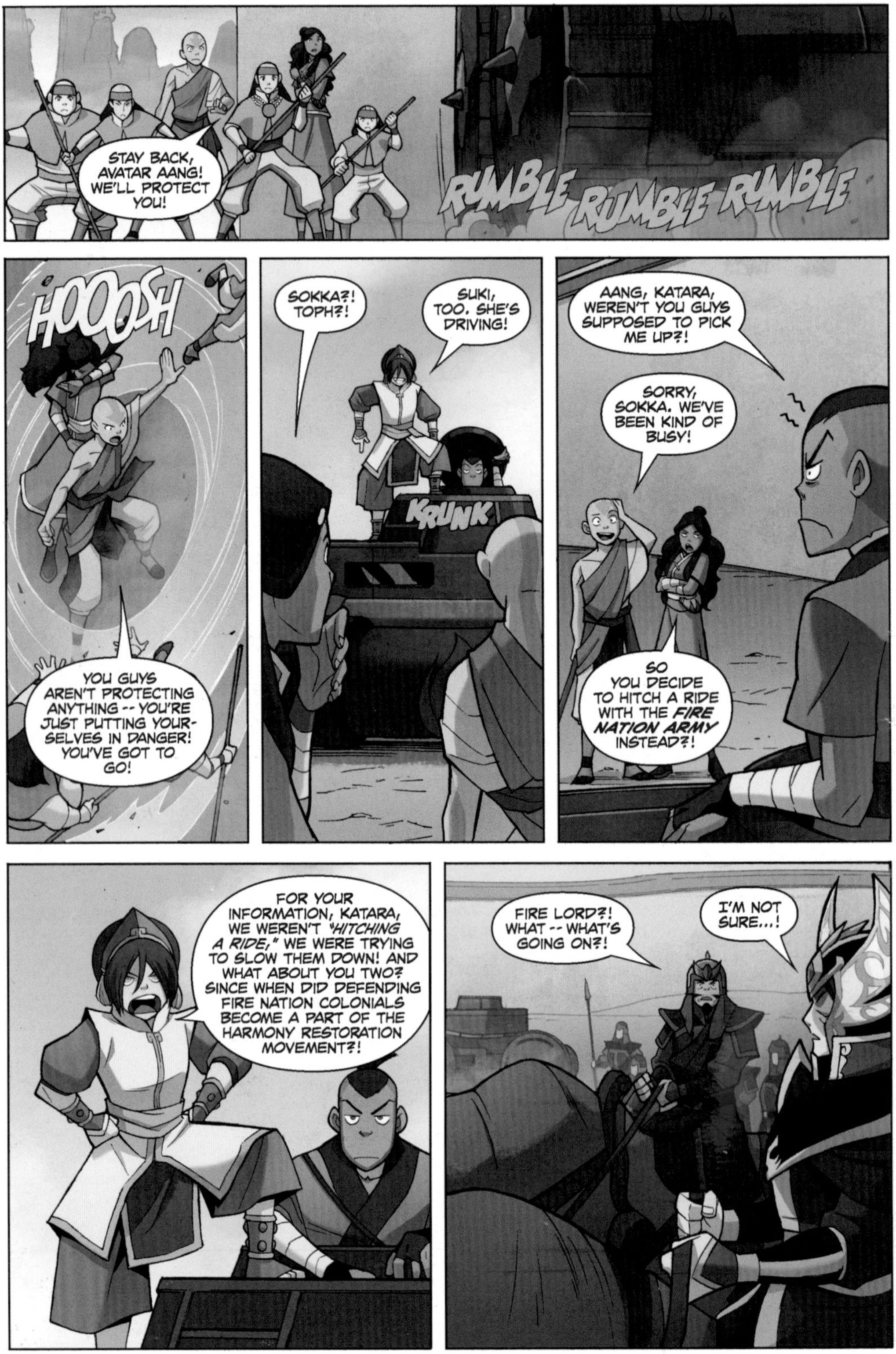
STAY BACK, AVATAR AANG! WE'LL PROTECT YOU!
RUMBLE RUMBLE RUMBLE
HOOOSH
YOU GUYS AREN'T PROTECTING ANYTHING -- YOU'RE JUST PUTTING YOURSELVES IN DANGER! YOU'VE GOT TO GO!
SOKKA?! TOPH?!
SUKI, TOO. SHE'S DRIVING!
KRUNK
AANG, KATARA, WEREN'T YOU GUYS SUPPOSED TO PICK ME UP?!
SORRY, SOKKA. WE'VE BEEN KIND OF BUSY!
SO YOU DECIDE TO HITCH A RIDE WITH THE *FIRE NATION ARMY* INSTEAD?!
FOR YOUR INFORMATION, KATARA, WE WEREN'T *"HITCHING A RIDE,"* WE WERE TRYING TO SLOW THEM DOWN! AND WHAT ABOUT YOU TWO? SINCE WHEN DID DEFENDING FIRE NATION COLONIALS BECOME A PART OF THE HARMONY RESTORATION MOVEMENT?!
FIRE LORD?! WHAT -- WHAT'S GOING ON?!
I'M NOT SURE...!

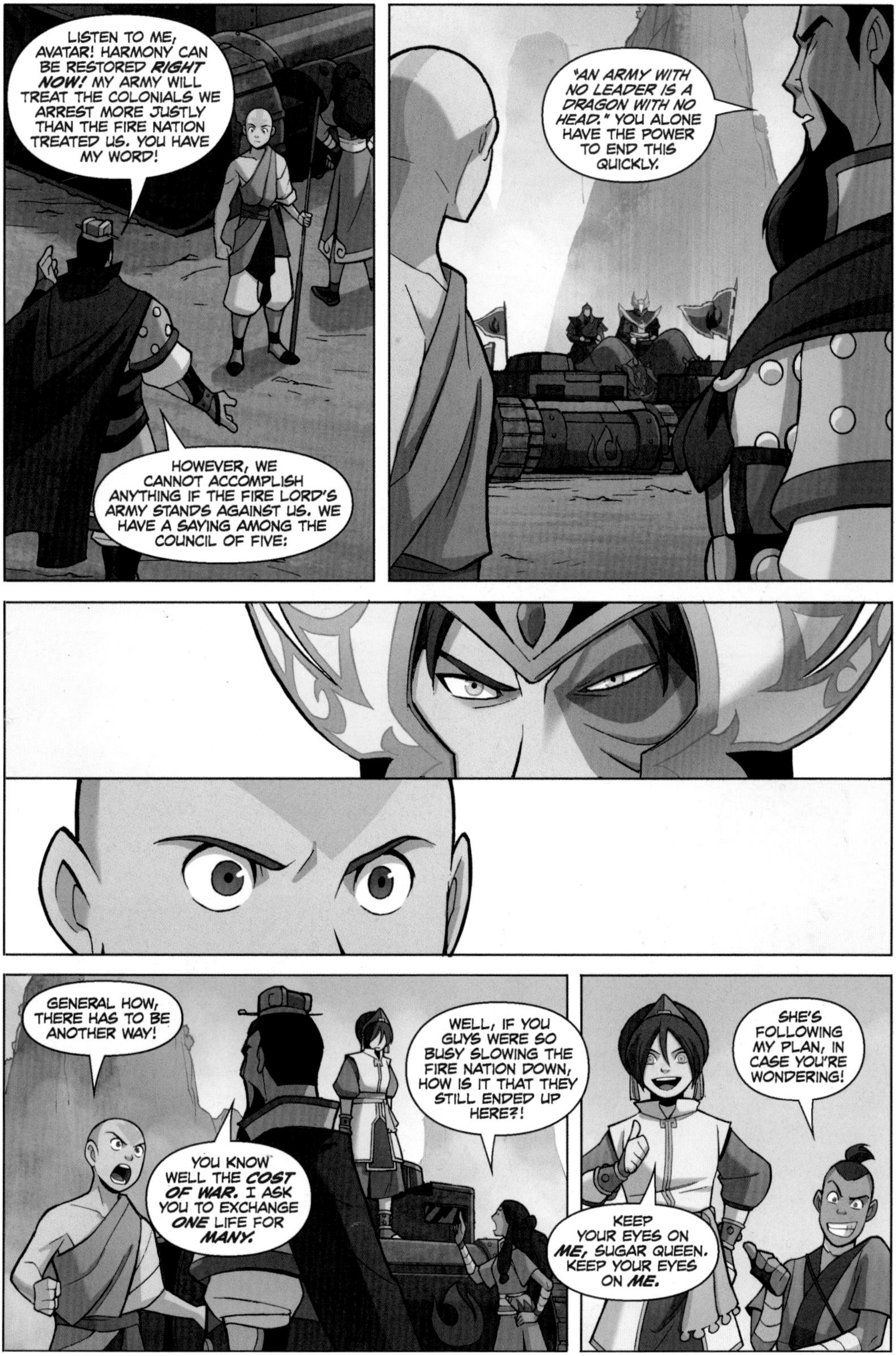
LISTEN TO ME, AVATAR! HARMONY CAN BE RESTORED RIGHT NOW! MY ARMY WILL TREAT THE COLONIALS WE ARREST MORE JUSTLY THAN THE FIRE NATION TREATED US. YOU HAVE MY WORD!
HOWEVER, WE CANNOT ACCOMPLISH ANYTHING IF THE FIRE LORD'S ARMY STANDS AGAINST US. WE HAVE A SAYING AMONG THE COUNCIL OF FIVE:
"AN ARMY WITH NO LEADER IS A DRAGON WITH NO HEAD." YOU ALONE HAVE THE POWER TO END THIS QUICKLY.
GENERAL HOW, THERE HAS TO BE ANOTHER WAY!
YOU KNOW WELL THE COST OF WAR. I ASK YOU TO EXCHANGE ONE LIFE FOR MANY.
WELL, IF YOU GUYS WERE SO BUSY SLOWING THE FIRE NATION DOWN, HOW IS IT THAT THEY STILL ENDED UP HERE?!
SHE'S FOLLOWING MY PLAN, IN CASE YOU'RE WONDERING!
KEEP YOUR EYES ON ME, SUGAR QUEEN. KEEP YOUR EYES ON ME.

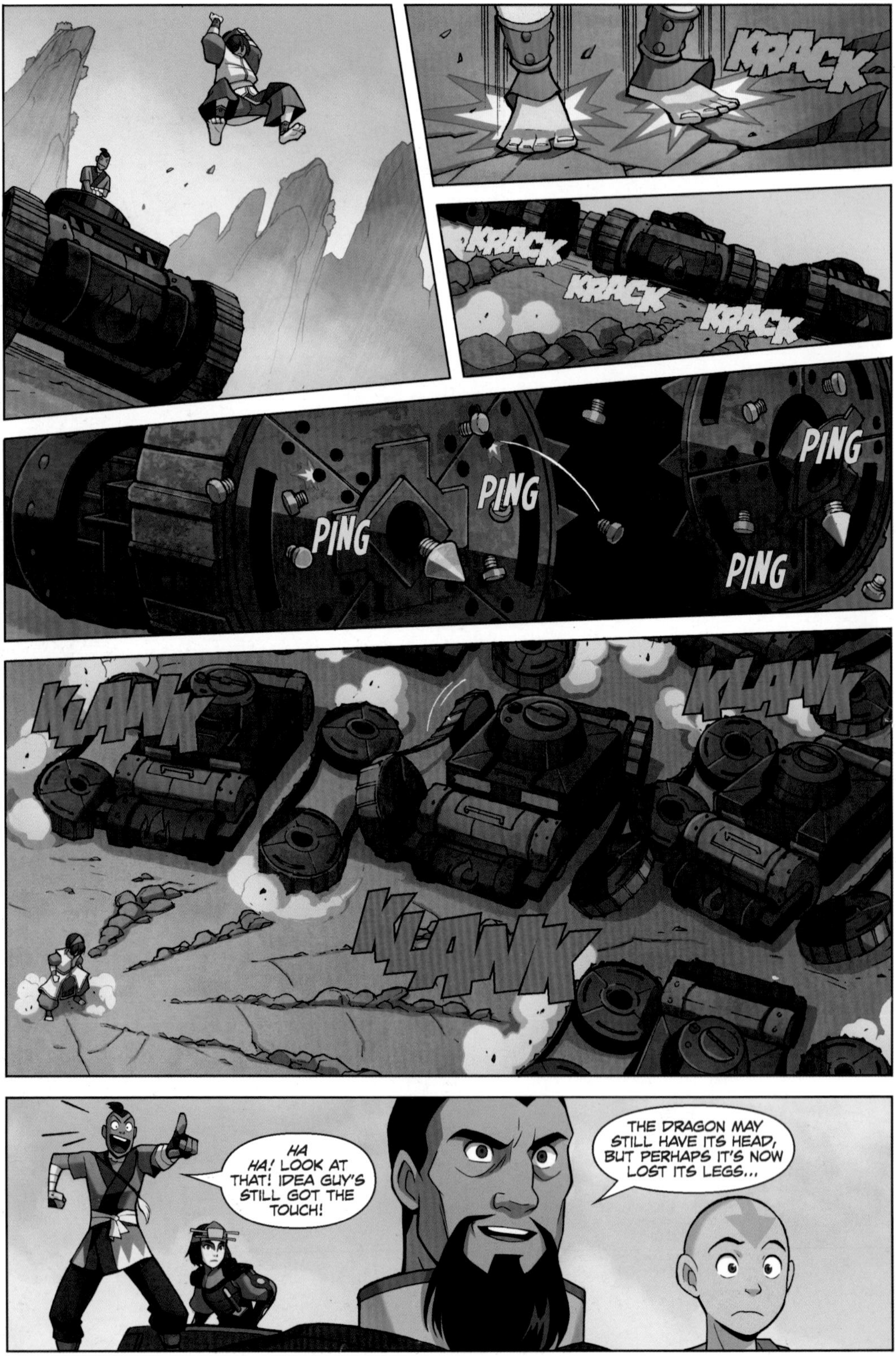

KRACK
KRACK
KRACK
KRACK
PING
PING
PING
PING
KLANK
KLANK
KLANK
HA HA! LOOK AT THAT! IDEA GUY'S STILL GOT THE TOUCH!
THE DRAGON MAY STILL HAVE ITS HEAD, BUT PERHAPS IT'S NOW LOST ITS LEGS...

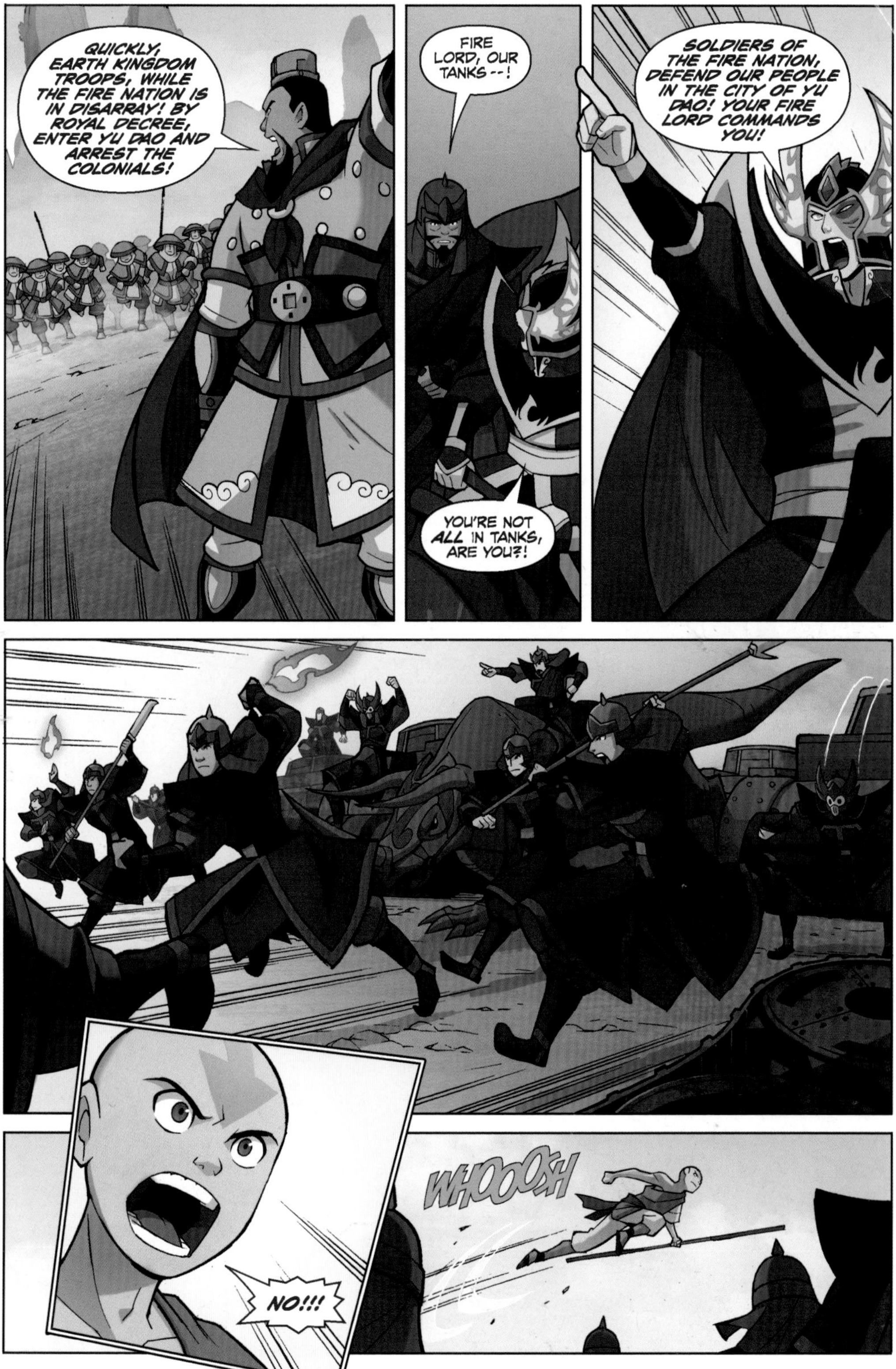
QUICKLY, EARTH KINGDOM TROOPS, WHILE THE FIRE NATION IS IN DISARRAY! BY ROYAL DECREE, ENTER YU DAO AND ARREST THE COLONIALS!
FIRE LORD, OUR TANKS--!
YOU'RE NOT ALL IN TANKS, ARE YOU?!
SOLDIERS OF THE FIRE NATION, DEFEND OUR PEOPLE IN THE CITY OF YU DAO! YOUR FIRE LORD COMMANDS YOU!
NO!!!
WHOOOSH

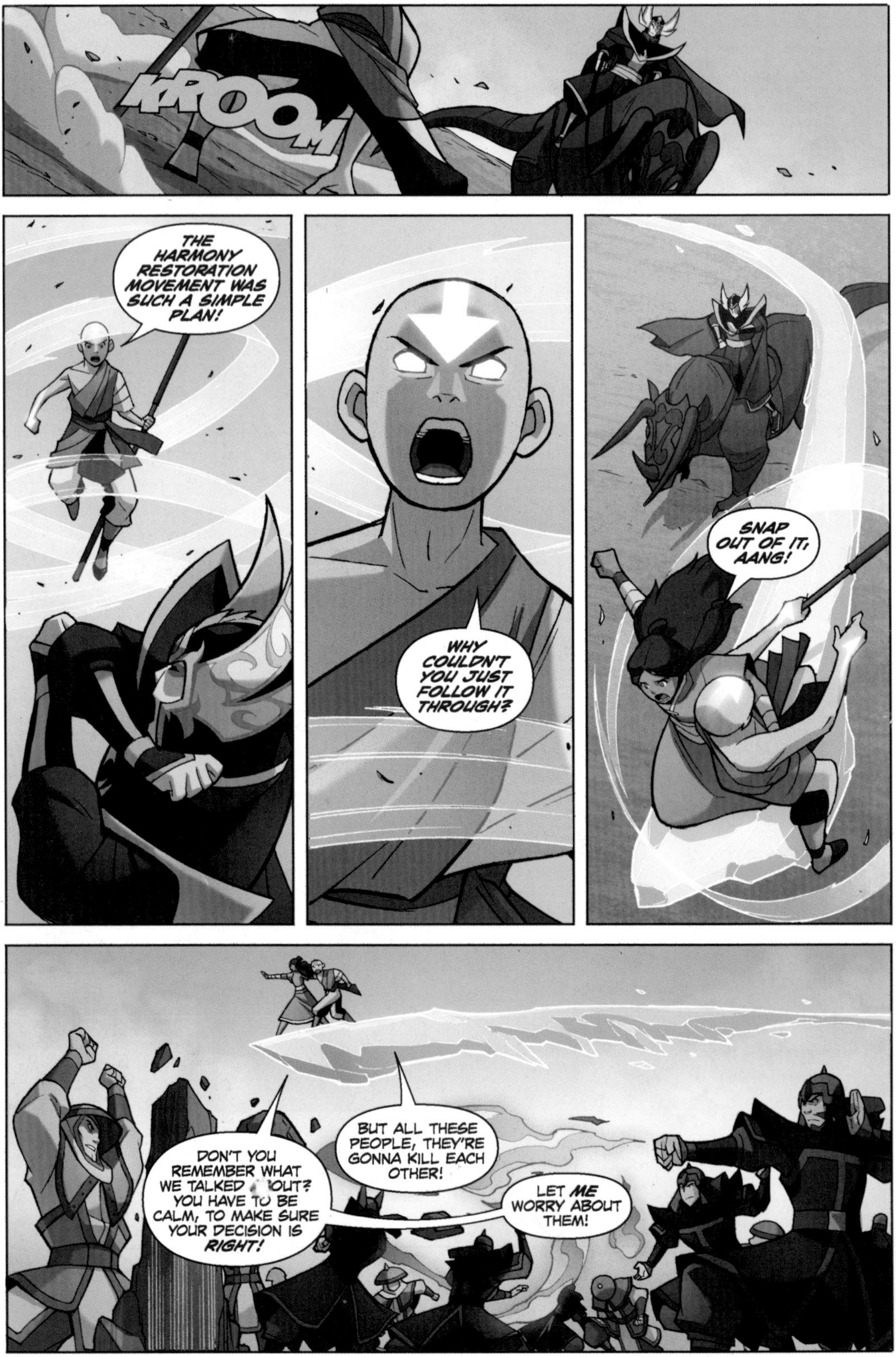
KROOM
THE HARMONY RESTORATION MOVEMENT WAS SUCH A SIMPLE PLAN!
WHY COULDN'T YOU JUST FOLLOW IT THROUGH?
SNAP OUT OF IT, AANG!
BUT ALL THESE PEOPLE, THEY'RE GONNA KILL EACH OTHER!
LET ME WORRY ABOUT THEM!
DON'T YOU REMEMBER WHAT WE TALKED ABOUT? YOU HAVE TO BE CALM, TO MAKE SURE YOUR DECISION IS RIGHT!

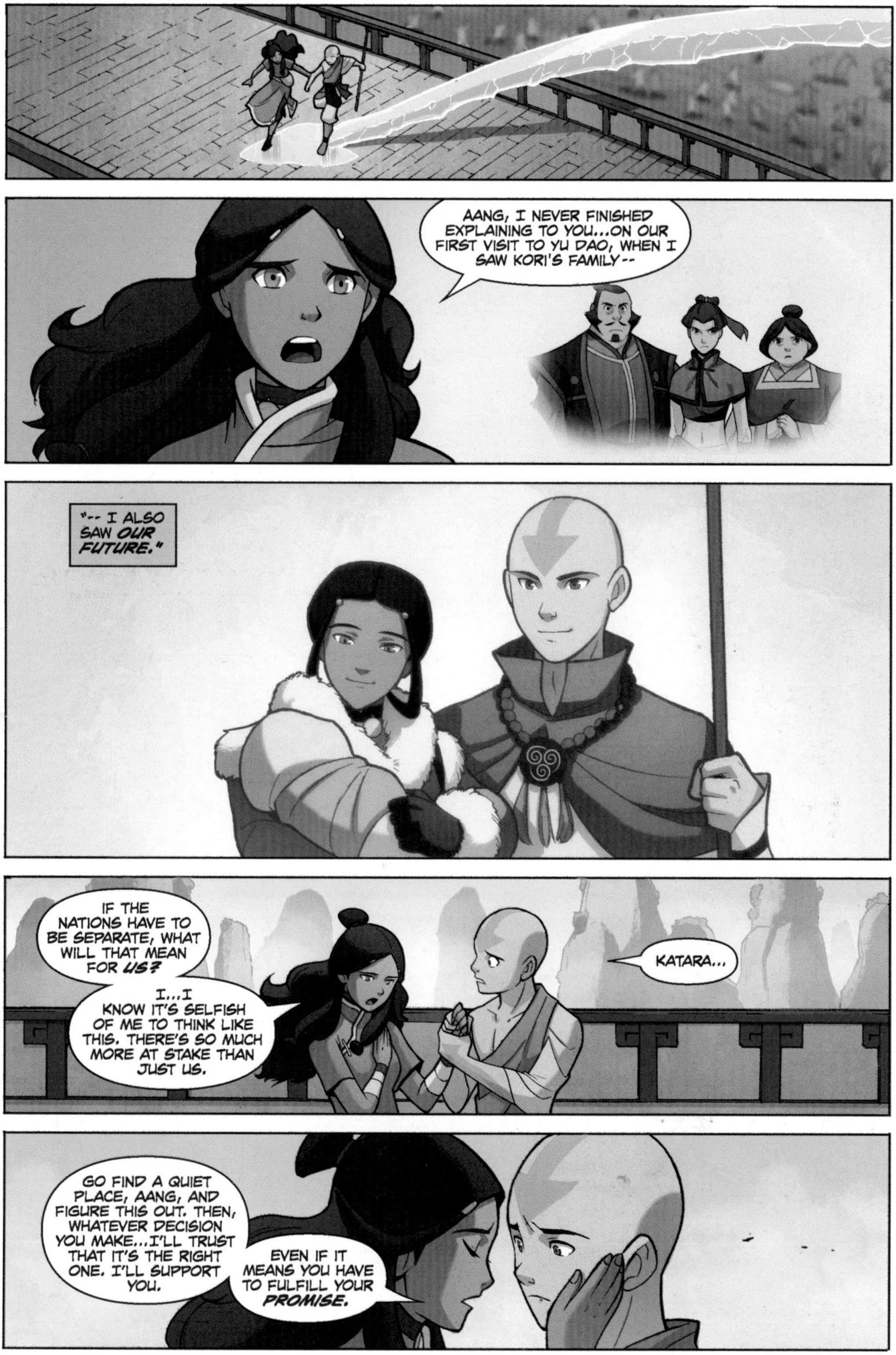
AANG, I NEVER FINISHED EXPLAINING TO YOU...ON OUR FIRST VISIT TO YU DAO, WHEN I SAW KORI'S FAMILY--
"-- I ALSO SAW *OUR FUTURE.*"
IF THE NATIONS HAVE TO BE SEPARATE, WHAT WILL THAT MEAN FOR *US?*
I...I KNOW IT'S SELFISH OF ME TO THINK LIKE THIS. THERE'S SO MUCH MORE AT STAKE THAN JUST US.
KATARA...
GO FIND A QUIET PLACE, AANG, AND FIGURE THIS OUT. THEN, WHATEVER DECISION YOU MAKE...I'LL TRUST THAT IT'S THE RIGHT ONE. I'LL SUPPORT YOU.
EVEN IF IT MEANS YOU HAVE TO FULFILL YOUR *PROMISE.*

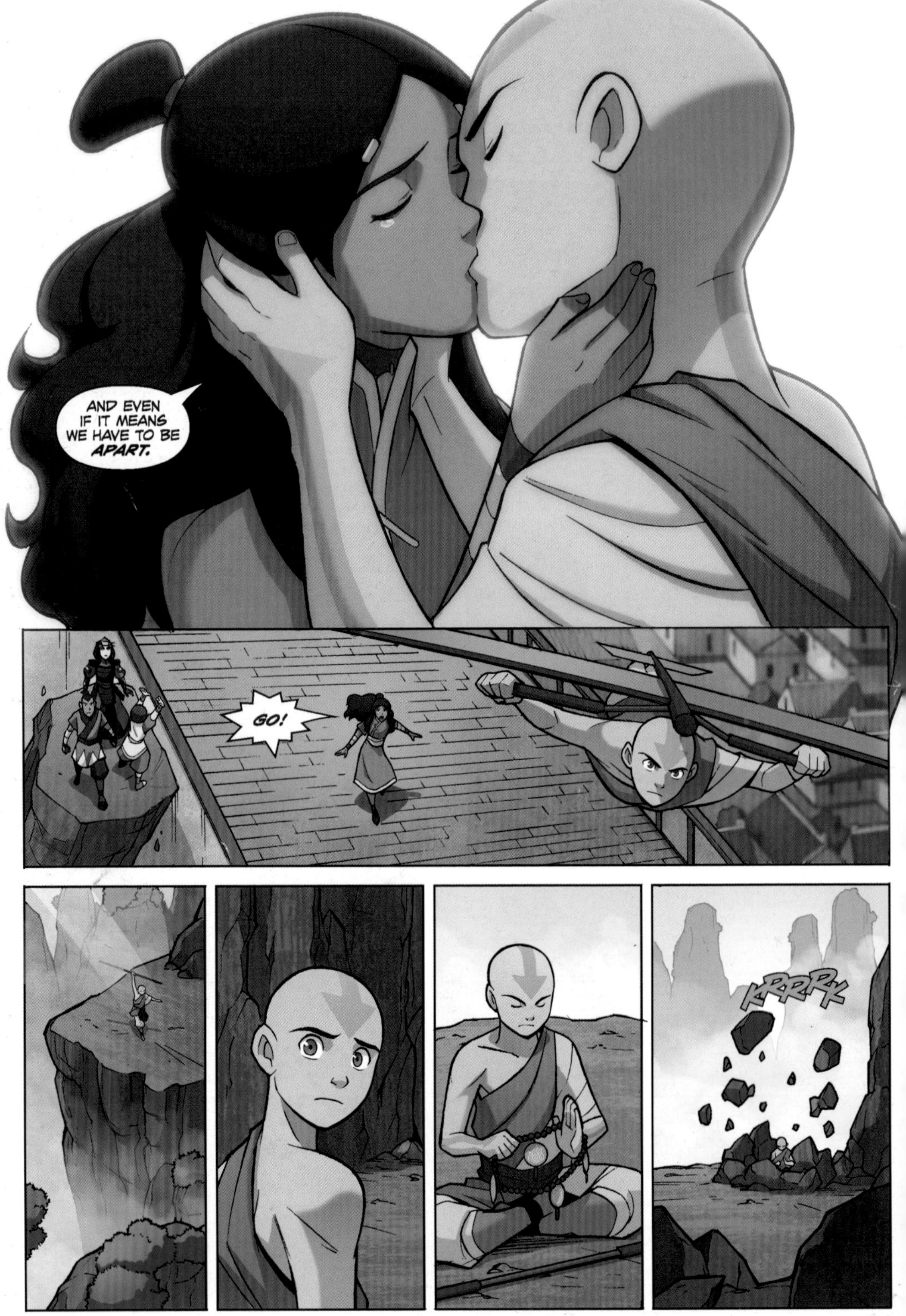
AND EVEN IF IT MEANS WE HAVE TO BE *APART.*
GO!
KRRRK

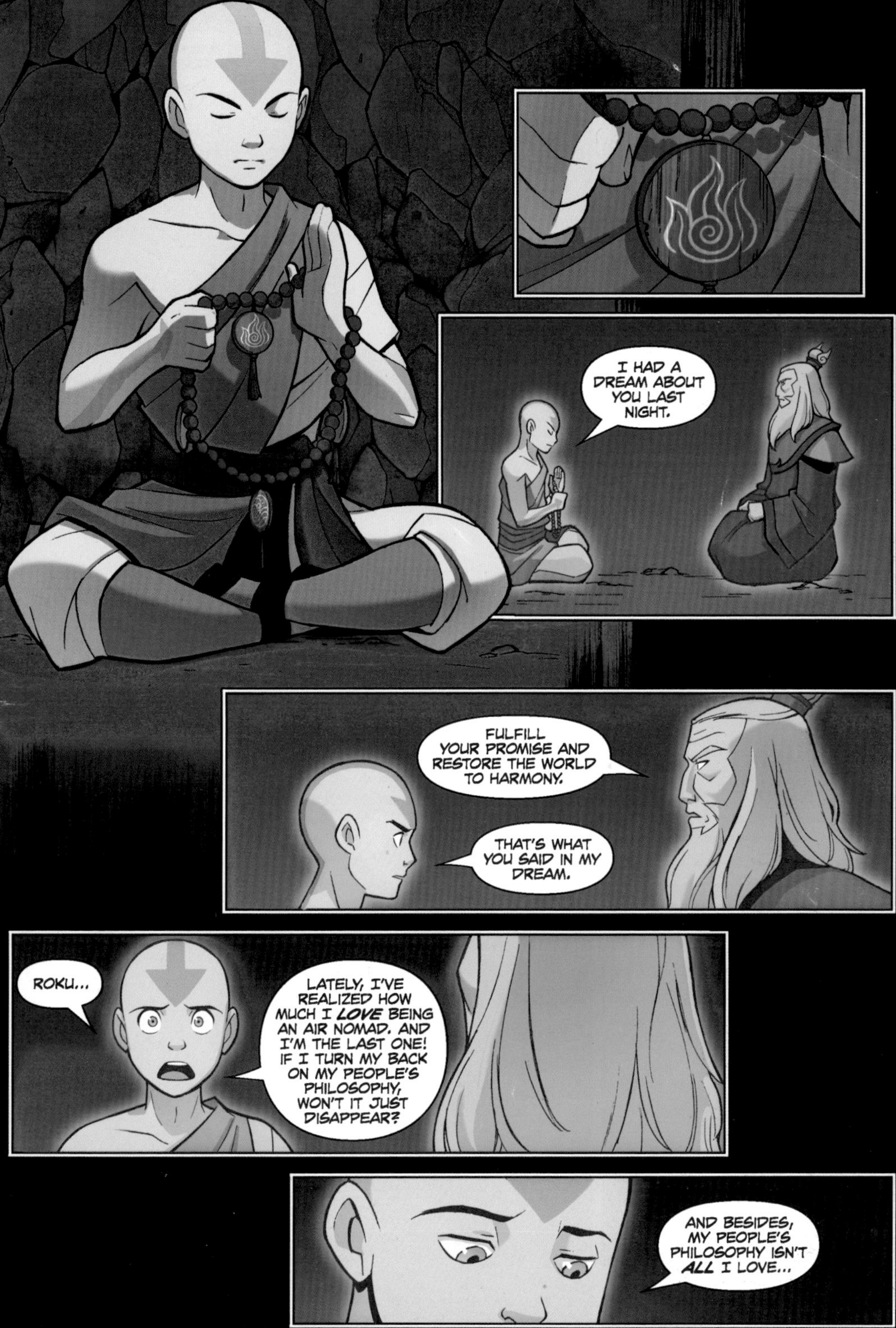
I HAD A DREAM ABOUT YOU LAST NIGHT.
FULFILL YOUR PROMISE AND RESTORE THE WORLD TO HARMONY.
THAT'S WHAT YOU SAID IN MY DREAM.
ROKU...
LATELY, I'VE REALIZED HOW MUCH I *LOVE* BEING AN AIR NOMAD. AND I'M THE LAST ONE! IF I TURN MY BACK ON MY PEOPLE'S PHILOSOPHY, WON'T IT JUST DISAPPEAR?
AND BESIDES, MY PEOPLE'S PHILOSOPHY ISN'T *ALL* I LOVE...

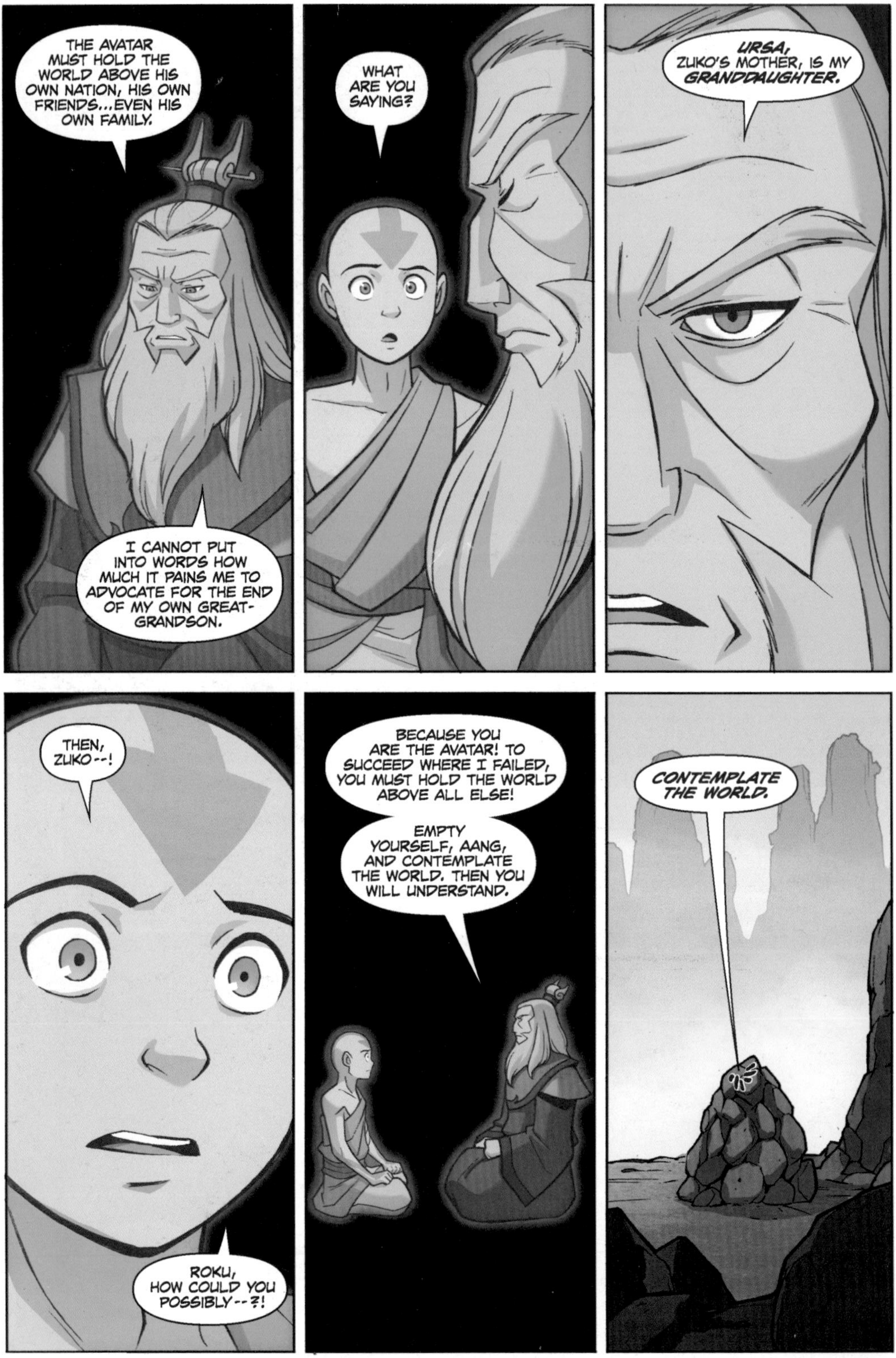
THE AVATAR MUST HOLD THE WORLD ABOVE HIS OWN NATION, HIS OWN FRIENDS...EVEN HIS OWN FAMILY.
I CANNOT PUT INTO WORDS HOW MUCH IT PAINS ME TO ADVOCATE FOR THE END OF MY OWN GREAT-GRANDSON.
WHAT ARE YOU SAYING?
URSA, ZUKO'S MOTHER, IS MY GRANDDAUGHTER.
THEN, ZUKO--!
ROKU, HOW COULD YOU POSSIBLY--?!
BECAUSE YOU ARE THE AVATAR! TO SUCCEED WHERE I FAILED, YOU MUST HOLD THE WORLD ABOVE ALL ELSE!
EMPTY YOURSELF, AANG, AND CONTEMPLATE THE WORLD. THEN YOU WILL UNDERSTAND.
CONTEMPLATE THE WORLD.

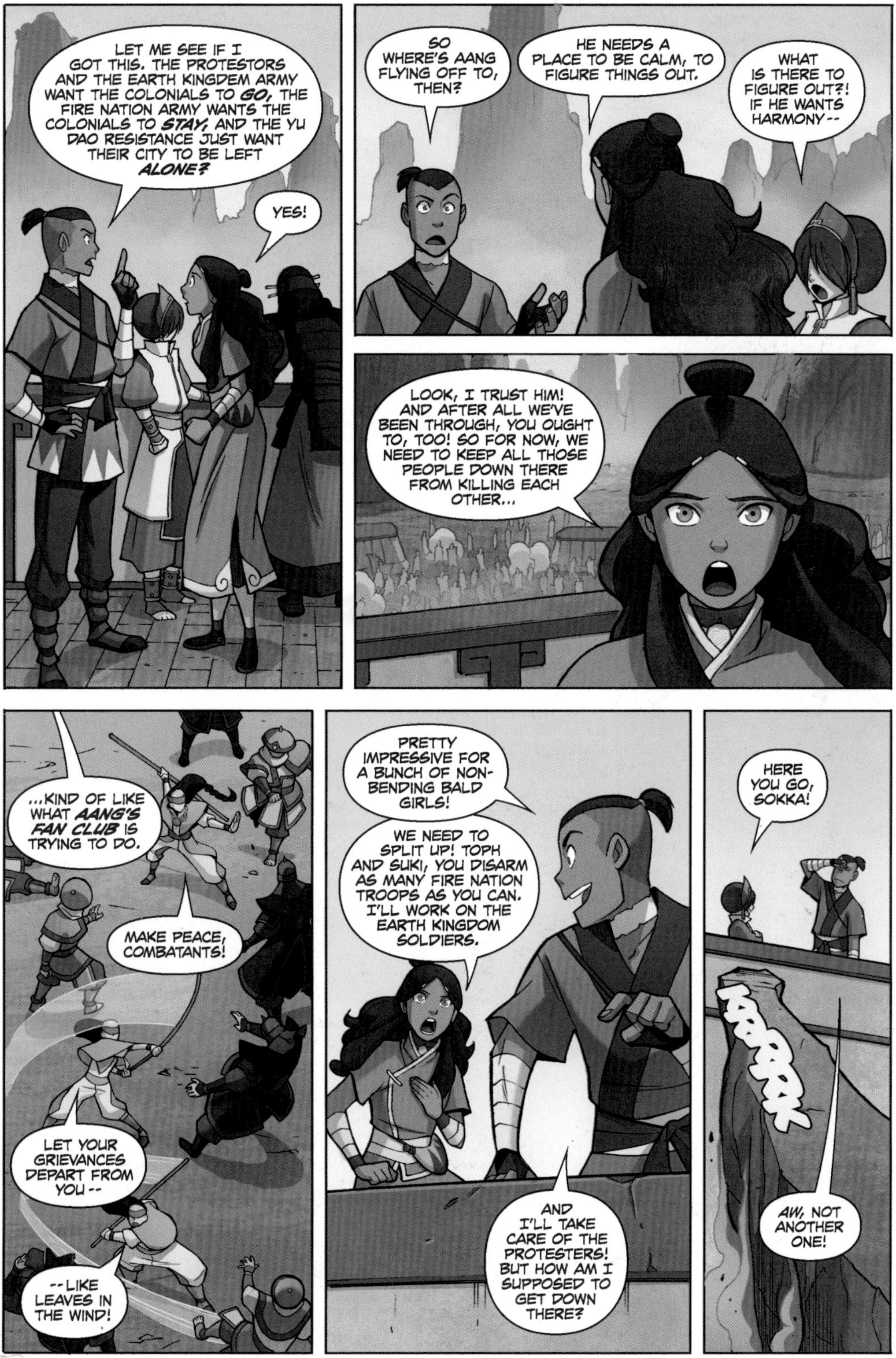
LET ME SEE IF I GOT THIS. THE PROTESTORS AND THE EARTH KINGDEM ARMY WANT THE COLONIALS TO GO, THE FIRE NATION ARMY WANTS THE COLONIALS TO STAY, AND THE YU DAO RESISTANCE JUST WANT THEIR CITY TO BE LEFT ALONE?
YES!
SO WHERE'S AANG FLYING OFF TO, THEN?
HE NEEDS A PLACE TO BE CALM, TO FIGURE THINGS OUT.
WHAT IS THERE TO FIGURE OUT?! IF HE WANTS HARMONY--
LOOK, I TRUST HIM! AND AFTER ALL WE'VE BEEN THROUGH, YOU OUGHT TO, TOO! SO FOR NOW, WE NEED TO KEEP ALL THOSE PEOPLE DOWN THERE FROM KILLING EACH OTHER...
...KIND OF LIKE WHAT AANG'S FAN CLUB IS TRYING TO DO.
MAKE PEACE, COMBATANTS!
LET YOUR GRIEVANCES DEPART FROM YOU --
--LIKE LEAVES IN THE WIND!
PRETTY IMPRESSIVE FOR A BUNCH OF NON-BENDING BALD GIRLS!
WE NEED TO SPLIT UP! TOPH AND SUKI, YOU DISARM AS MANY FIRE NATION TROOPS AS YOU CAN. I'LL WORK ON THE EARTH KINGDOM SOLDIERS.
AND I'LL TAKE CARE OF THE PROTESTERS! BUT HOW AM I SUPPOSED TO GET DOWN THERE?
HERE YOU GO, SOKKA!
KRRRRK
AW, NOT ANOTHER ONE!

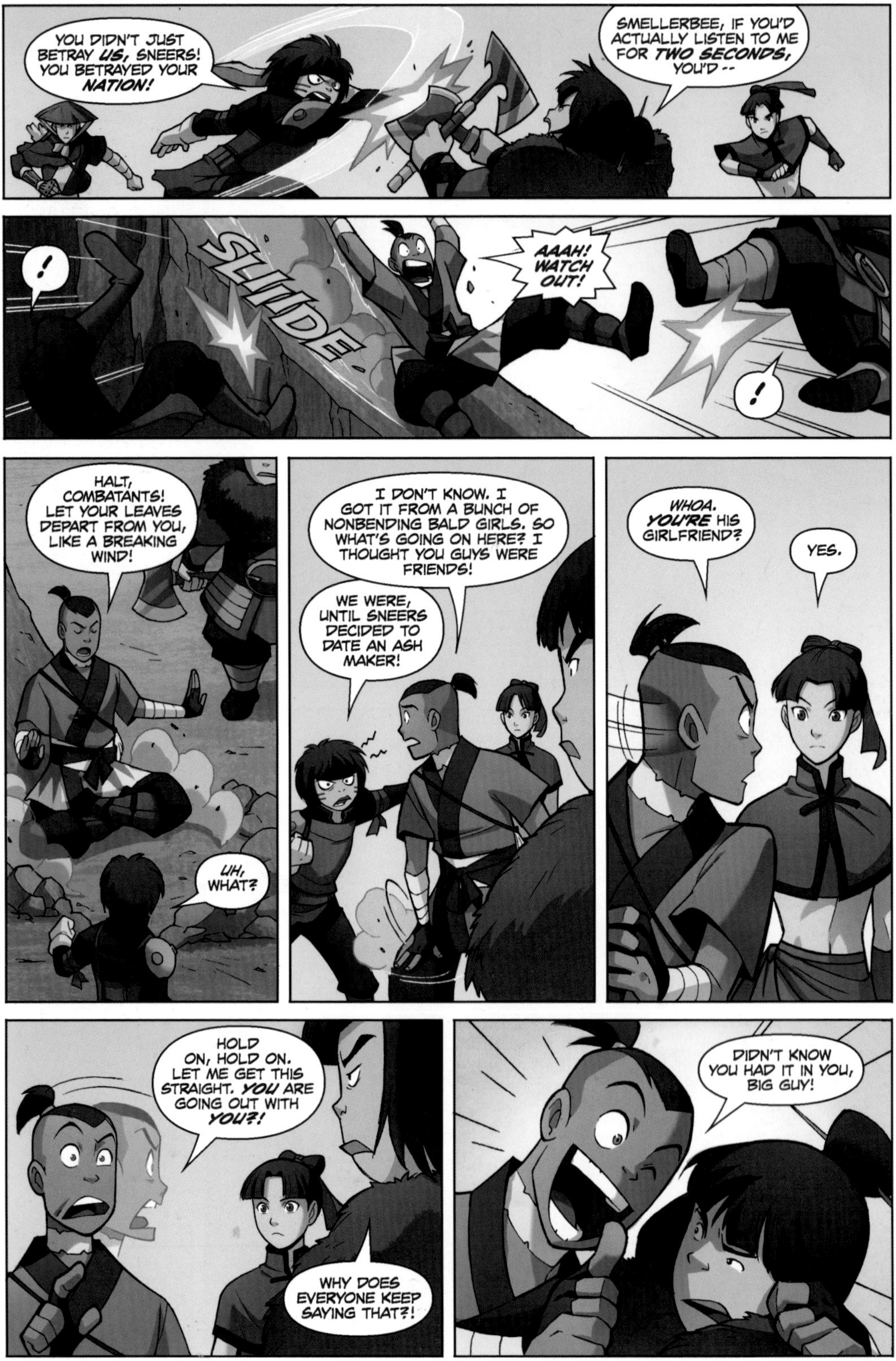
YOU DIDN'T JUST BETRAY *US*, SNEERS! YOU BETRAYED YOUR *NATION*!
SMELLERBEE, IF YOU'D ACTUALLY LISTEN TO ME FOR *TWO SECONDS*, YOU'D --
!
SLIIDE
AAAH! WATCH OUT!
!
HALT, COMBATANTS! LET YOUR LEAVES DEPART FROM YOU, LIKE A BREAKING WIND!
UH, WHAT?
I DON'T KNOW. I GOT IT FROM A BUNCH OF NONBENDING BALD GIRLS. SO WHAT'S GOING ON HERE? I THOUGHT YOU GUYS WERE FRIENDS!
WE WERE, UNTIL SNEERS DECIDED TO DATE AN ASH MAKER!
WHOA. YOU'RE HIS GIRLFRIEND?
YES.
HOLD ON, HOLD ON. LET ME GET THIS STRAIGHT. *YOU* ARE GOING OUT WITH *YOU*?!
WHY DOES EVERYONE KEEP SAYING THAT?!
DIDN'T KNOW YOU HAD IT IN YOU, BIG GUY!

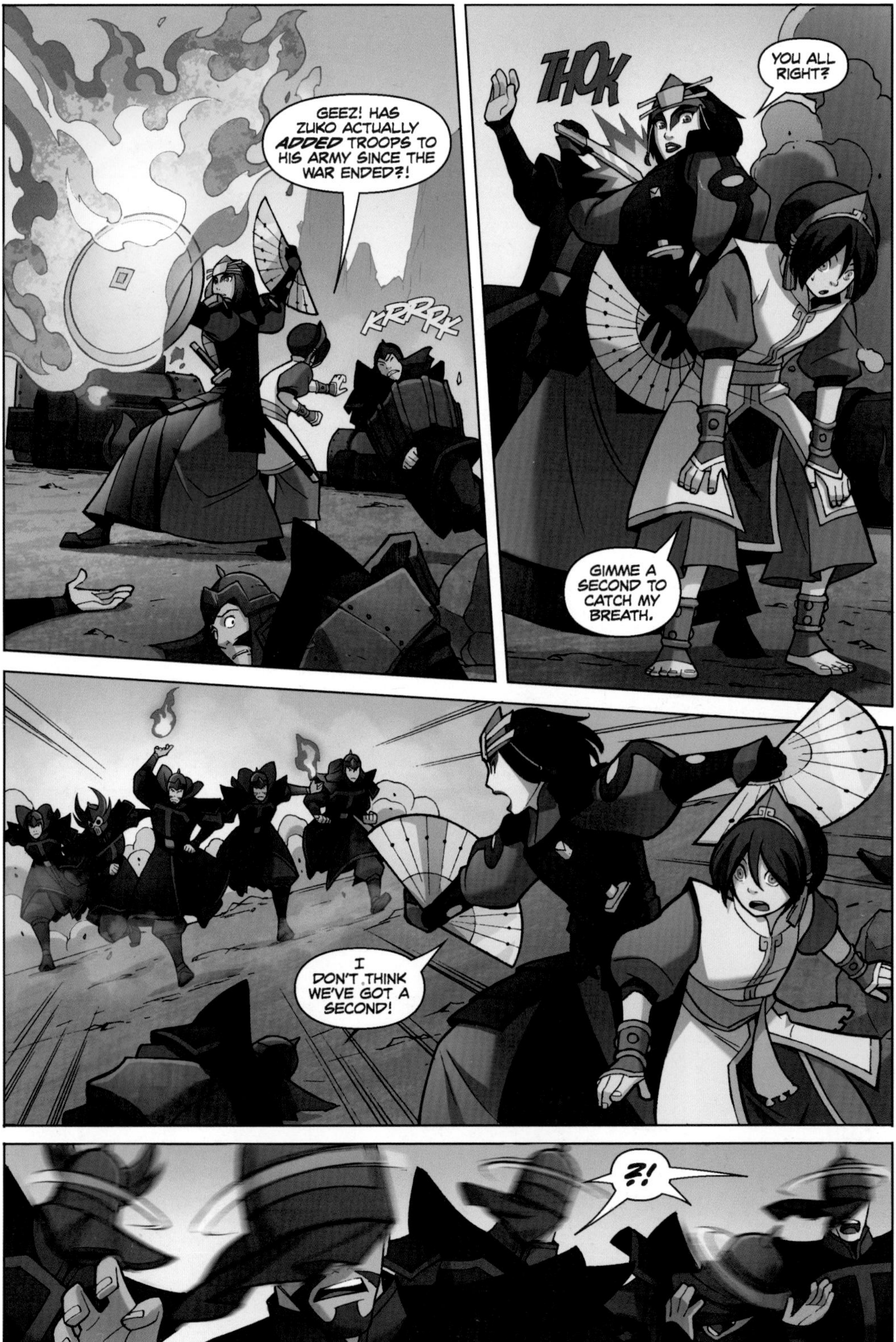
GEEZ! HAS ZUKO ACTUALLY ADDED TROOPS TO HIS ARMY SINCE THE WAR ENDED?!
KRRRK
THOK
YOU ALL RIGHT?
GIMME A SECOND TO CATCH MY BREATH.
I DON'T THINK WE'VE GOT A SECOND!
?!

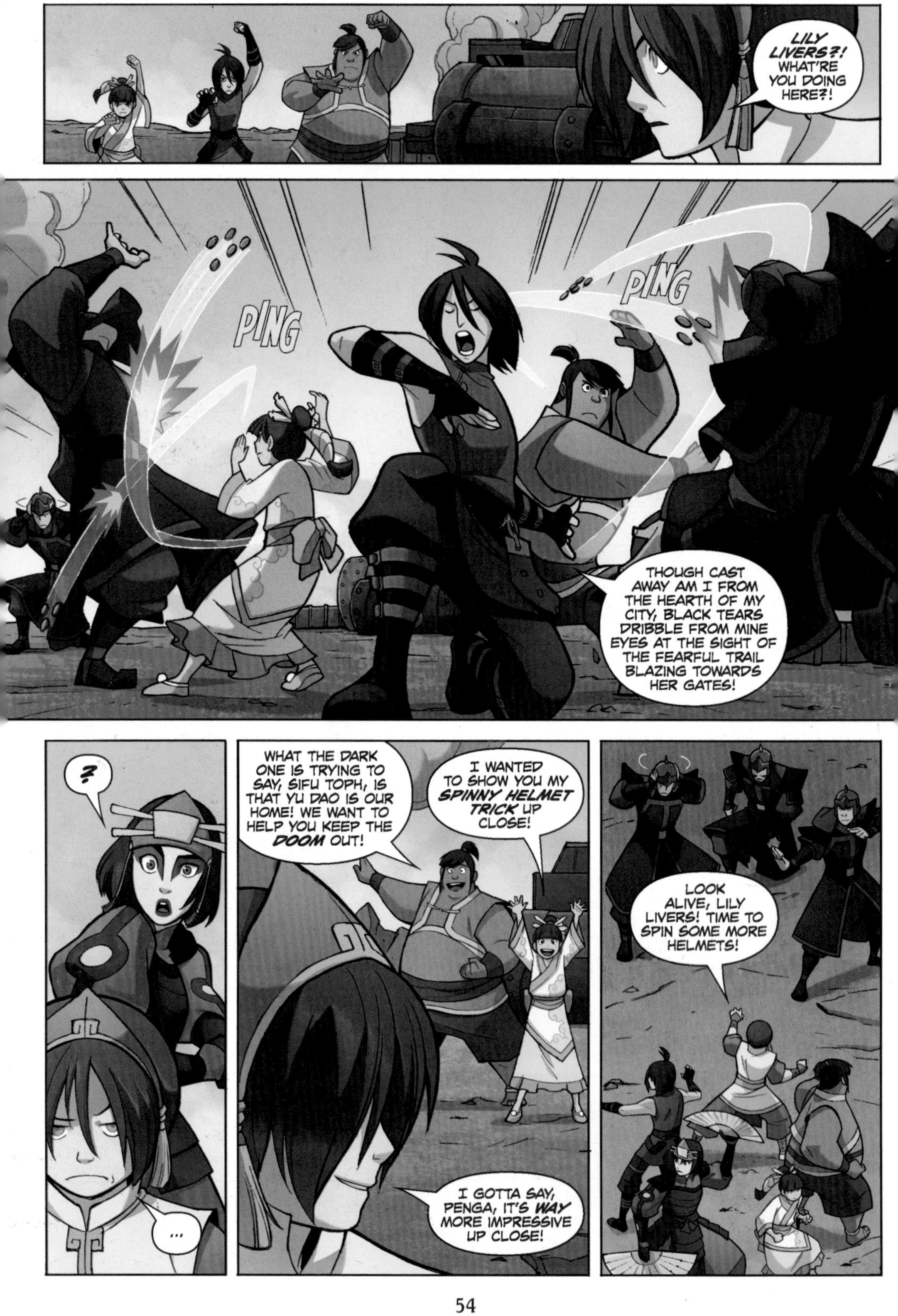
LILY LIVERS?! WHAT'RE YOU DOING HERE?!
PING
PING
THOUGH CAST AWAY AM I FROM THE HEARTH OF MY CITY, BLACK TEARS DRIBBLE FROM MINE EYES AT THE SIGHT OF THE FEARFUL TRAIL BLAZING TOWARDS HER GATES!
?
...
WHAT THE DARK ONE IS TRYING TO SAY, SIFU TOPH, IS THAT YU DAO IS OUR HOME! WE WANT TO HELP YOU KEEP THE DOOM OUT!
I WANTED TO SHOW YOU MY SPINNY HELMET TRICK UP CLOSE!
I GOTTA SAY, PENGA, IT'S WAY MORE IMPRESSIVE UP CLOSE!
LOOK ALIVE, LILY LIVERS! TIME TO SPIN SOME MORE HELMETS!

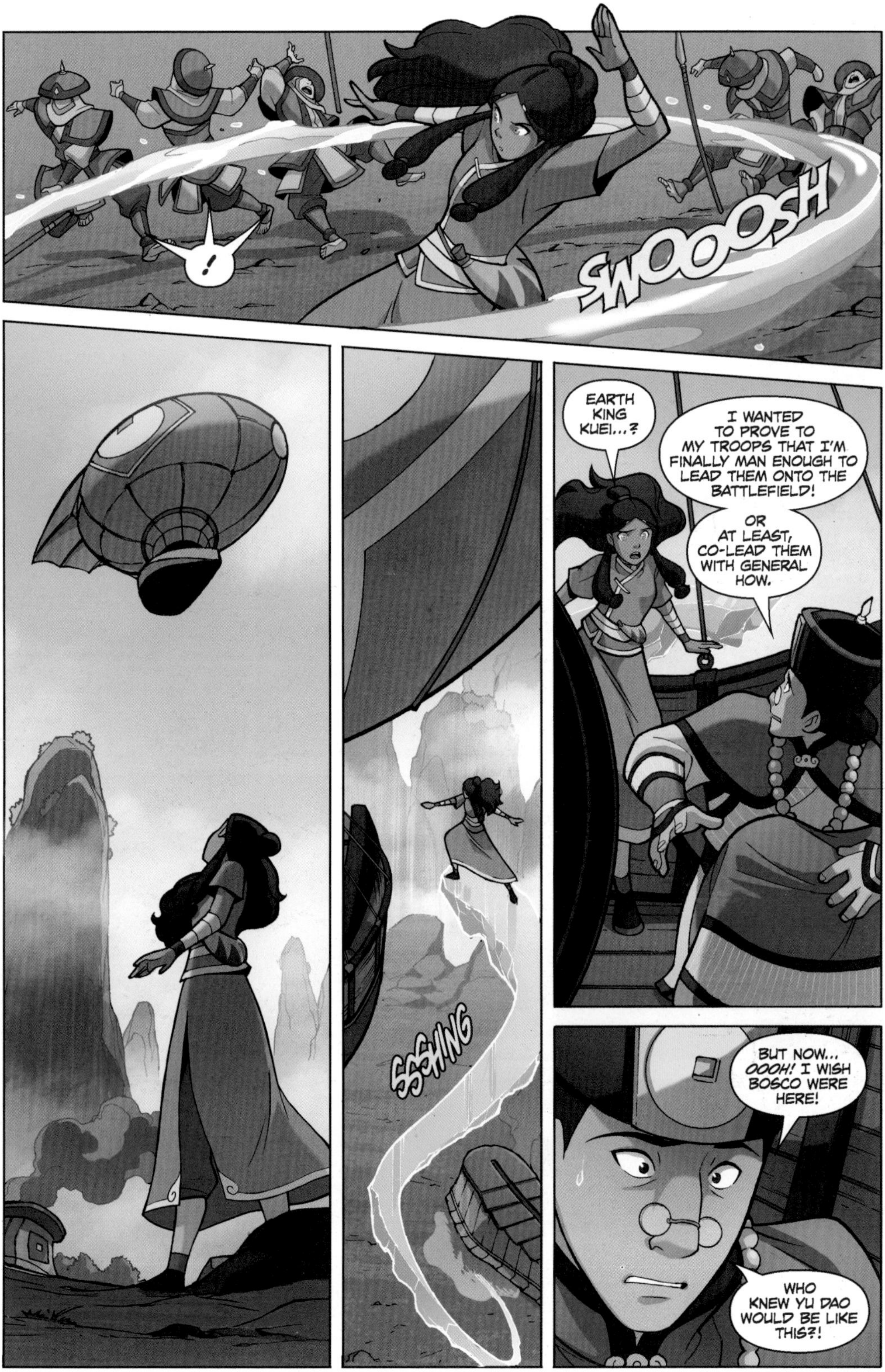

SWOOOSH
!
EARTH KING KUEI...?
I WANTED TO PROVE TO MY TROOPS THAT I'M FINALLY MAN ENOUGH TO LEAD THEM ONTO THE BATTLEFIELD!
OR AT LEAST, CO-LEAD THEM WITH GENERAL HOW.
SSSHING
BUT NOW... OOOH! I WISH BOSCO WERE HERE!
WHO KNEW YU DAO WOULD BE LIKE THIS?!

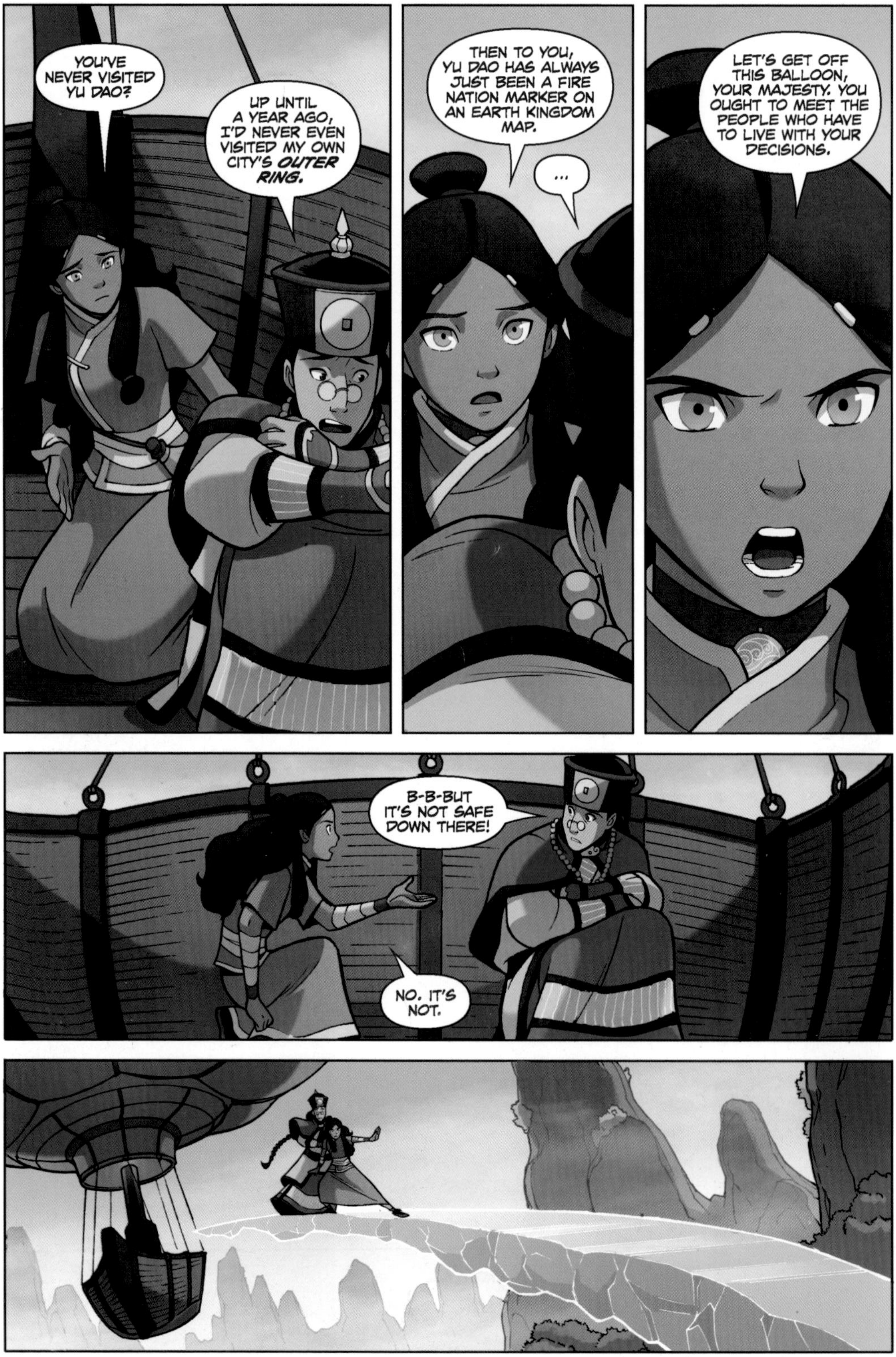
YOU'VE NEVER VISITED YU DAO?
UP UNTIL A YEAR AGO, I'D NEVER EVEN VISITED MY OWN CITY'S OUTER RING.
THEN TO YOU, YU DAO HAS ALWAYS JUST BEEN A FIRE NATION MARKER ON AN EARTH KINGDOM MAP.
...
LET'S GET OFF THIS BALLOON, YOUR MAJESTY. YOU OUGHT TO MEET THE PEOPLE WHO HAVE TO LIVE WITH YOUR DECISIONS.
B-B-BUT IT'S NOT SAFE DOWN THERE!
NO. IT'S NOT.

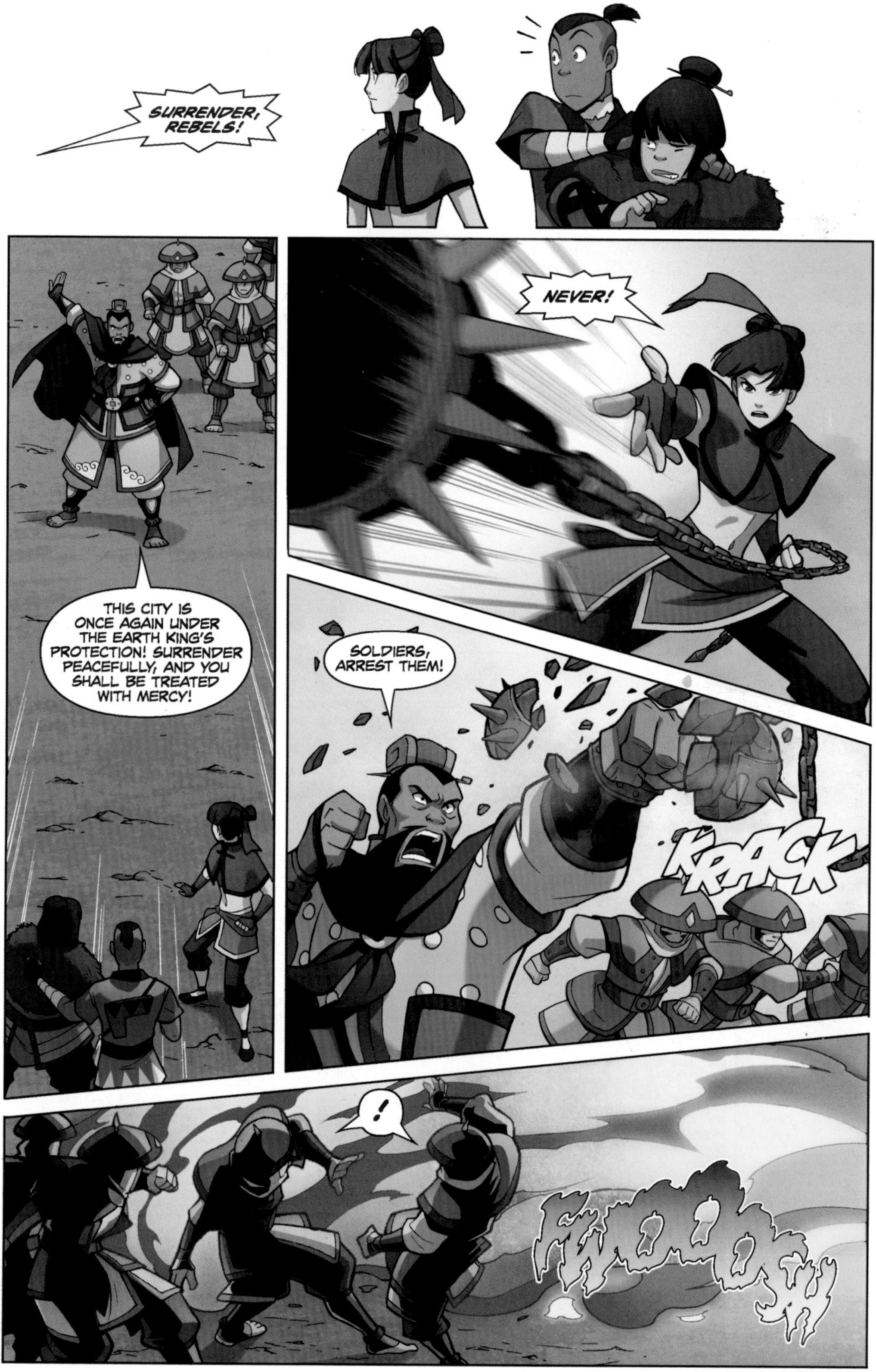
SURRENDER, REBELS!
THIS CITY IS ONCE AGAIN UNDER THE EARTH KING'S PROTECTION! SURRENDER PEACEFULLY, AND YOU SHALL BE TREATED WITH MERCY!
NEVER!
SOLDIERS, ARREST THEM!
KRACK
!
FWOOSH

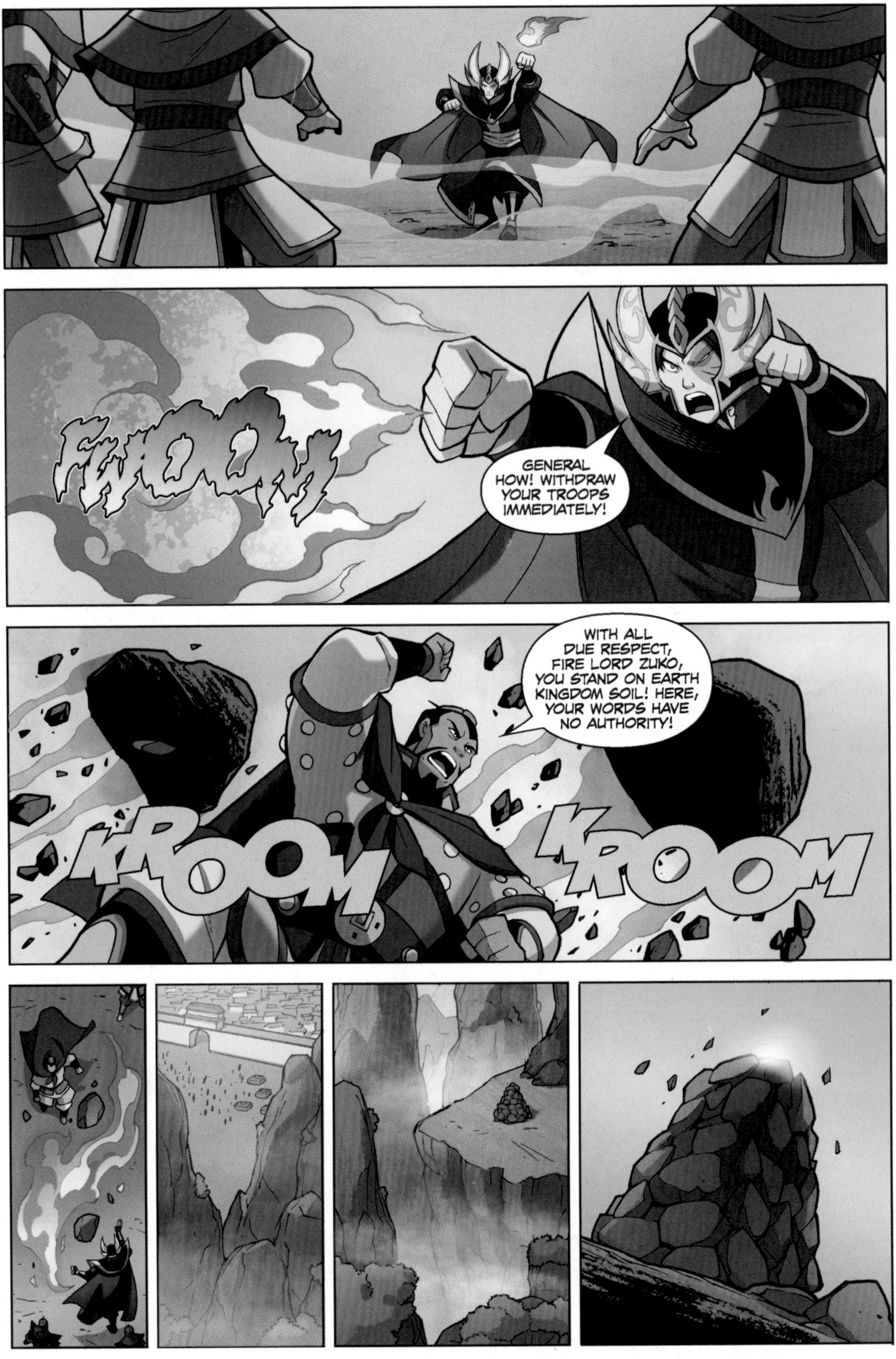
FWOOM
GENERAL HOW! WITHDRAW YOUR TROOPS IMMEDIATELY!
WITH ALL DUE RESPECT, FIRE LORD ZUKO, YOU STAND ON EARTH KINGDOM SOIL! HERE, YOUR WORDS HAVE NO AUTHORITY!
KROOM
KROOM

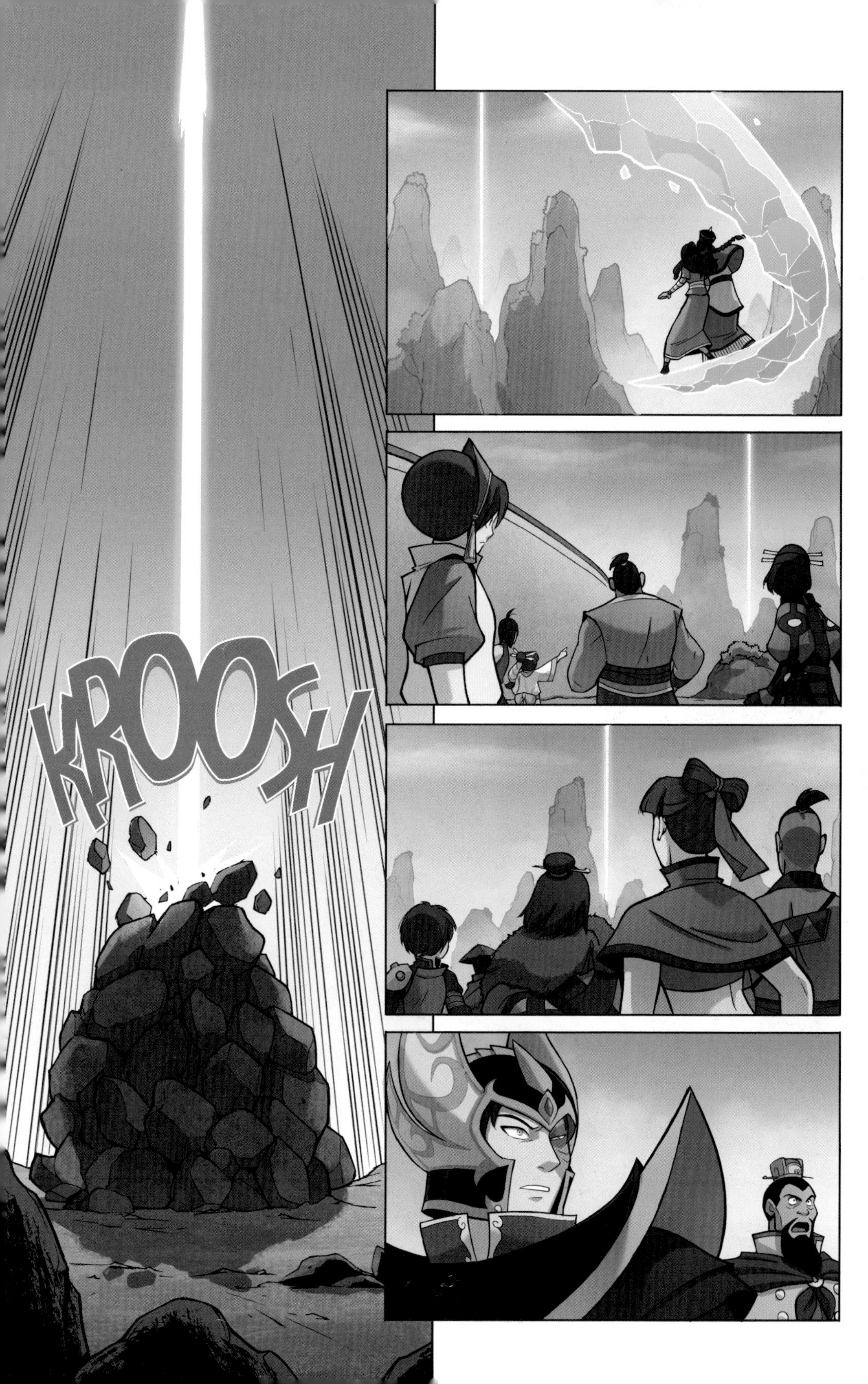
KROOSH

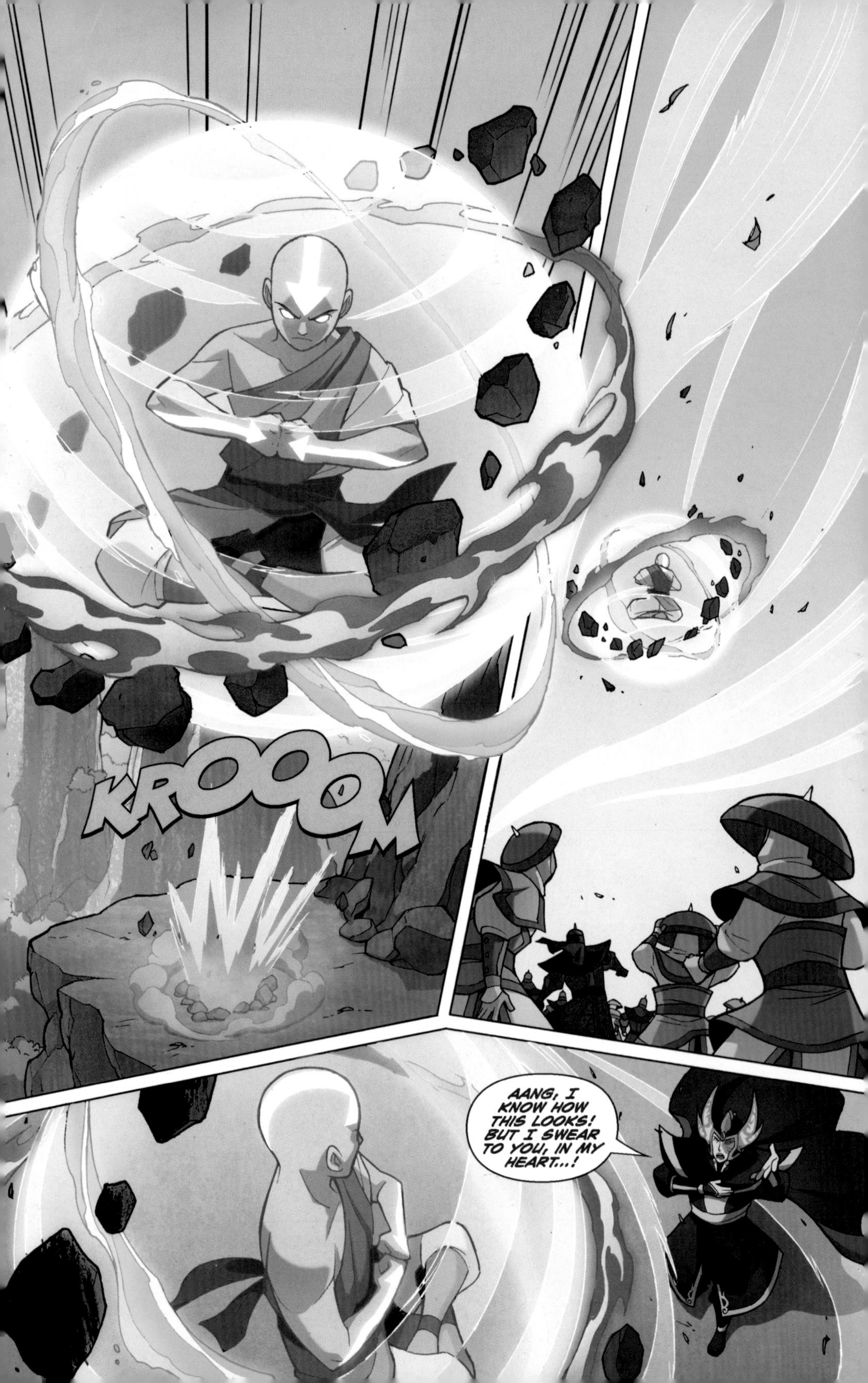
KROOOM
AANG, I KNOW HOW THIS LOOKS! BUT I SWEAR TO YOU, IN MY HEART...!

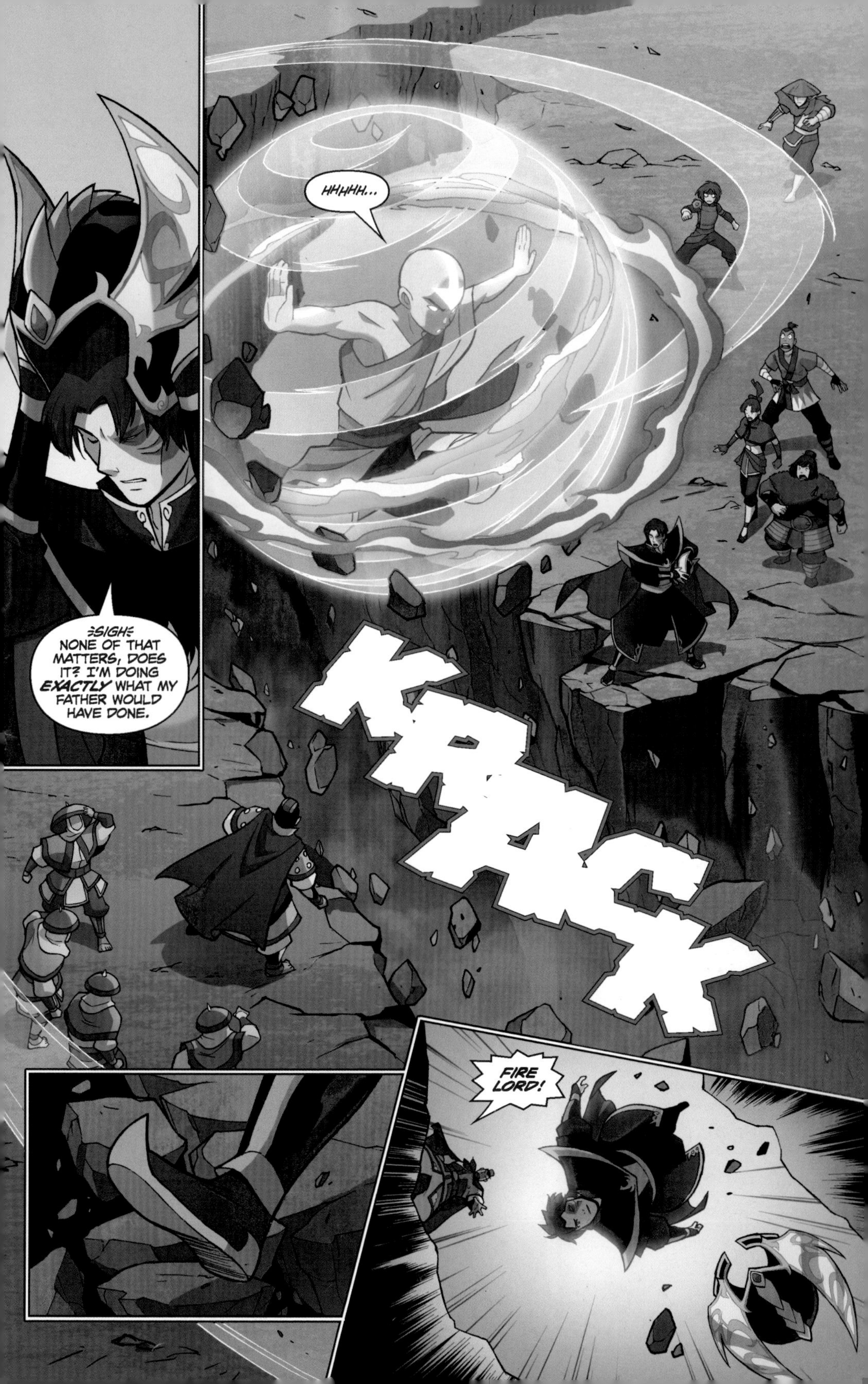

HHHHH...
SIGH
NONE OF THAT MATTERS, DOES IT? I'M DOING EXACTLY WHAT MY FATHER WOULD HAVE DONE.
KRACK
FIRE LORD!

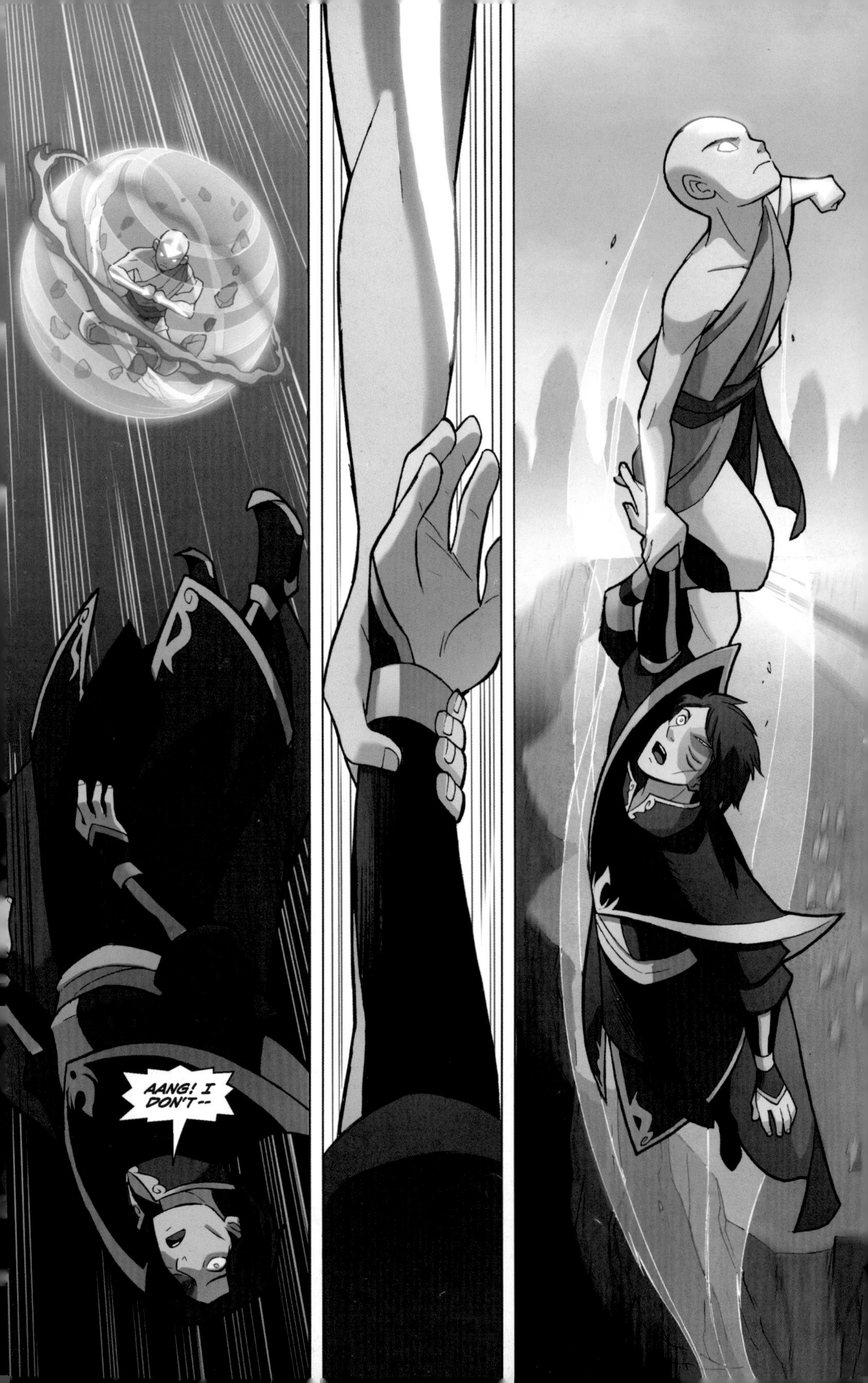
AANG! I DON'T--

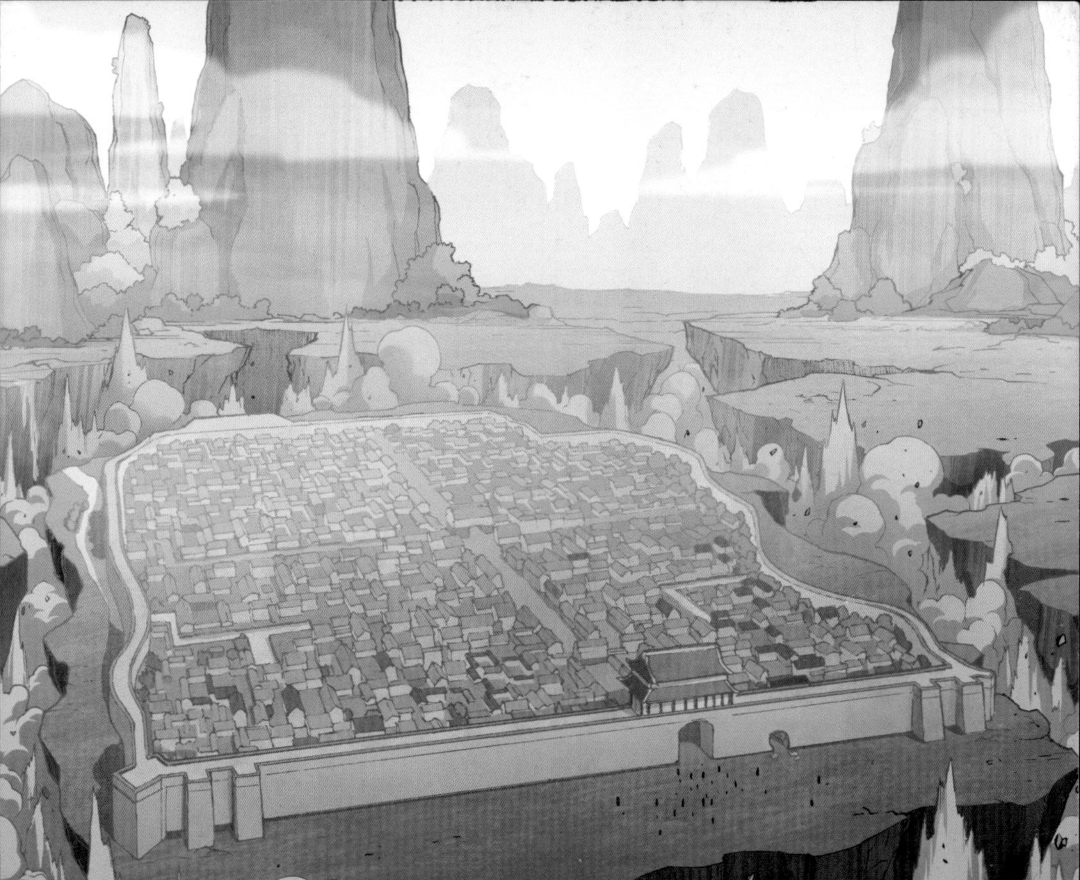

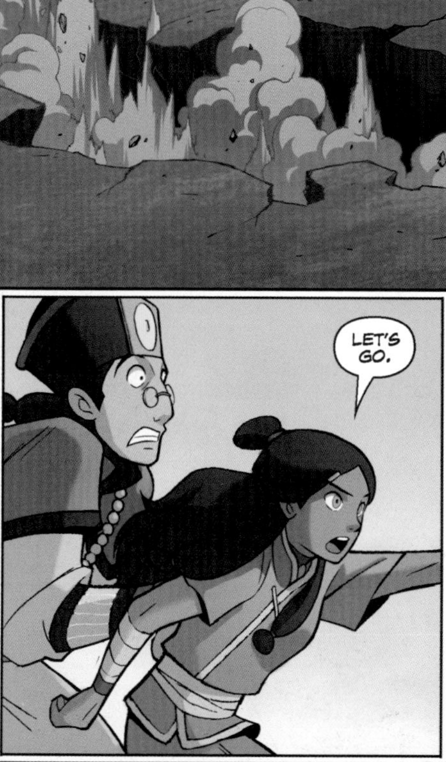
LET'S GO.

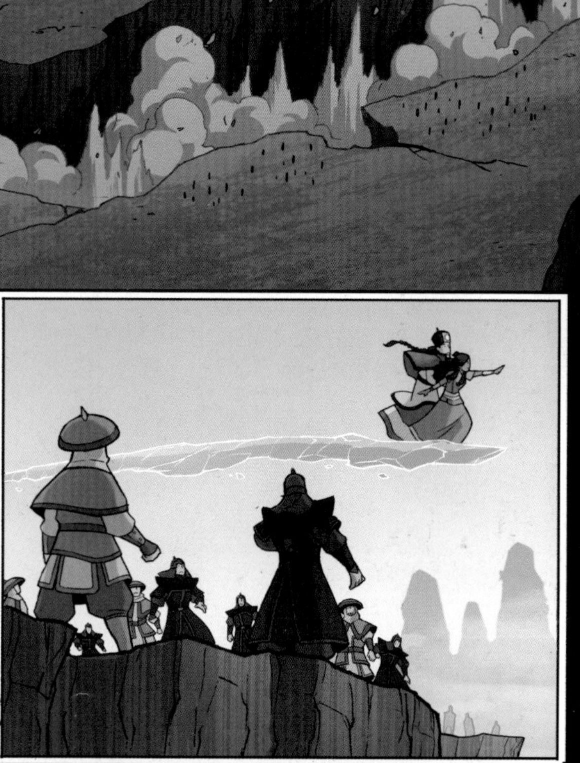

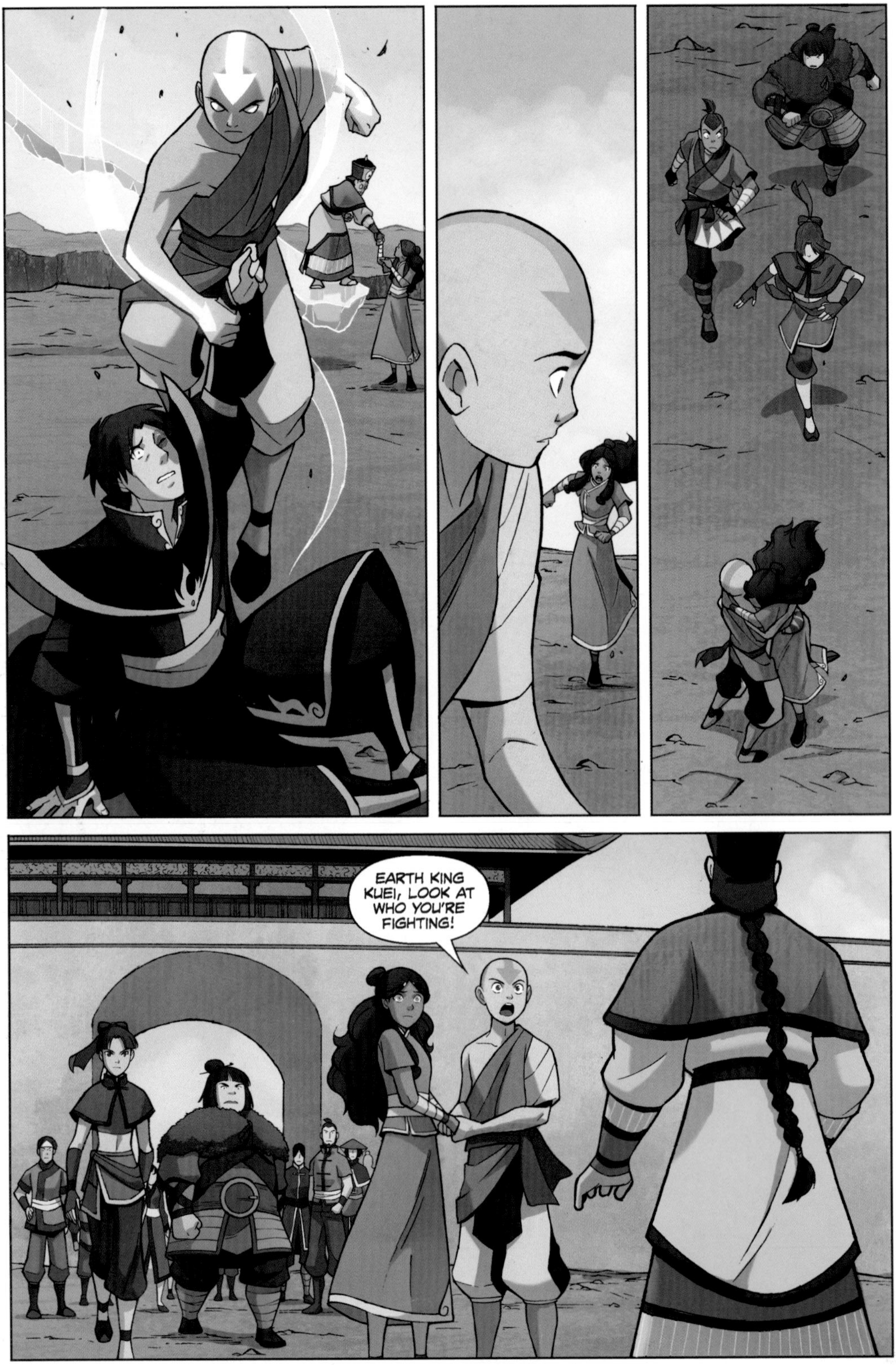
EARTH KING KUEI, LOOK AT WHO YOU'RE FIGHTING!

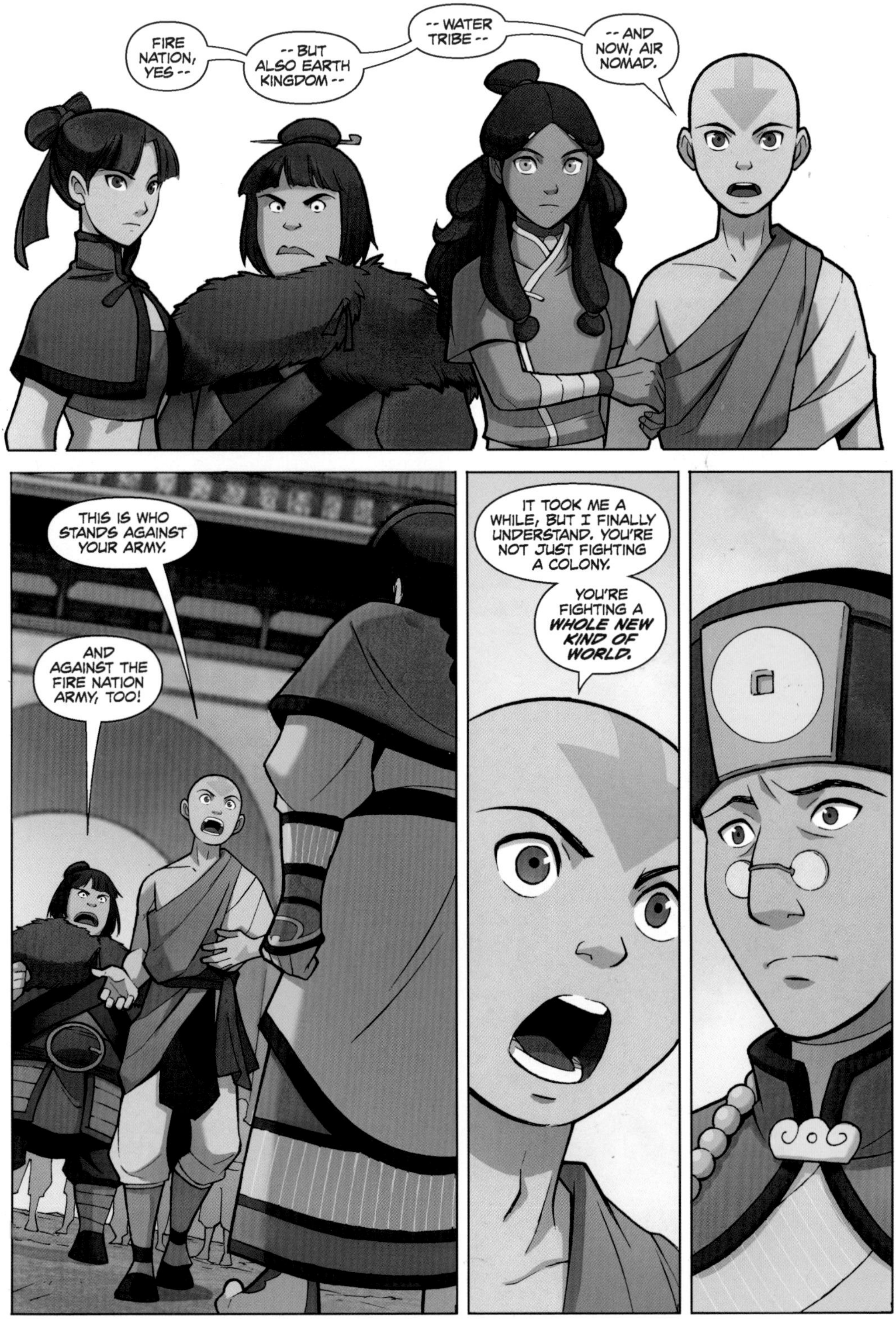
FIRE NATION, YES --
-- BUT ALSO EARTH KINGDOM --
-- WATER TRIBE --
-- AND NOW, AIR NOMAD.
THIS IS WHO STANDS AGAINST YOUR ARMY.
AND AGAINST THE FIRE NATION ARMY, TOO!
IT TOOK ME A WHILE, BUT I FINALLY UNDERSTAND. YOU'RE NOT JUST FIGHTING A COLONY.
YOU'RE FIGHTING A *WHOLE NEW KIND OF WORLD.*

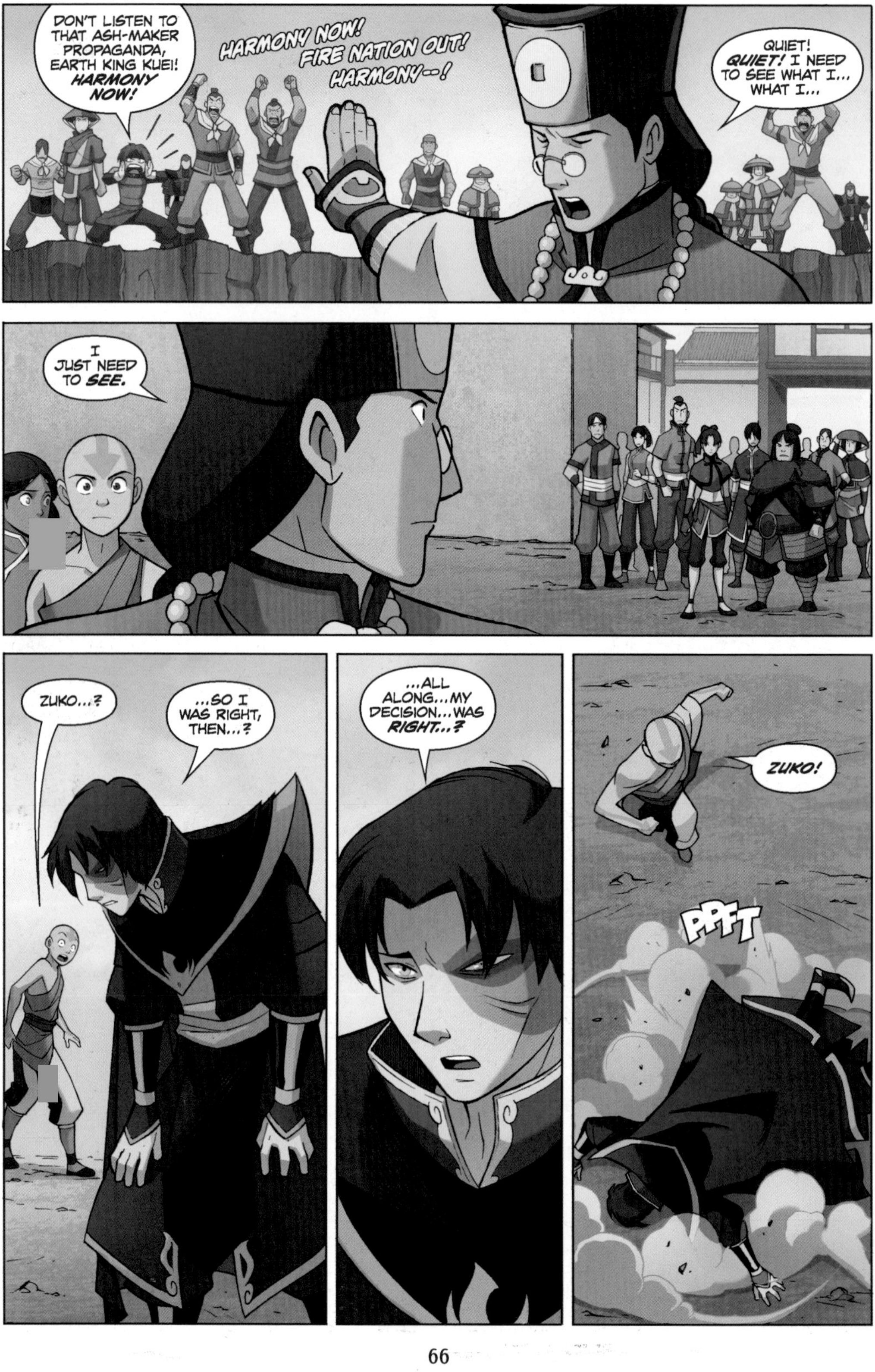
DON'T LISTEN TO THAT ASH-MAKER PROPAGANDA, EARTH KING KUEI! HARMONY NOW!
HARMONY NOW! FIRE NATION OUT! HARMONY--!
QUIET! QUIET! I NEED TO SEE WHAT I... WHAT I...
I JUST NEED TO SEE.
ZUKO...?
...SO I WAS RIGHT, THEN...?
...ALL ALONG...MY DECISION...WAS RIGHT...?
ZUKO!
PPFT

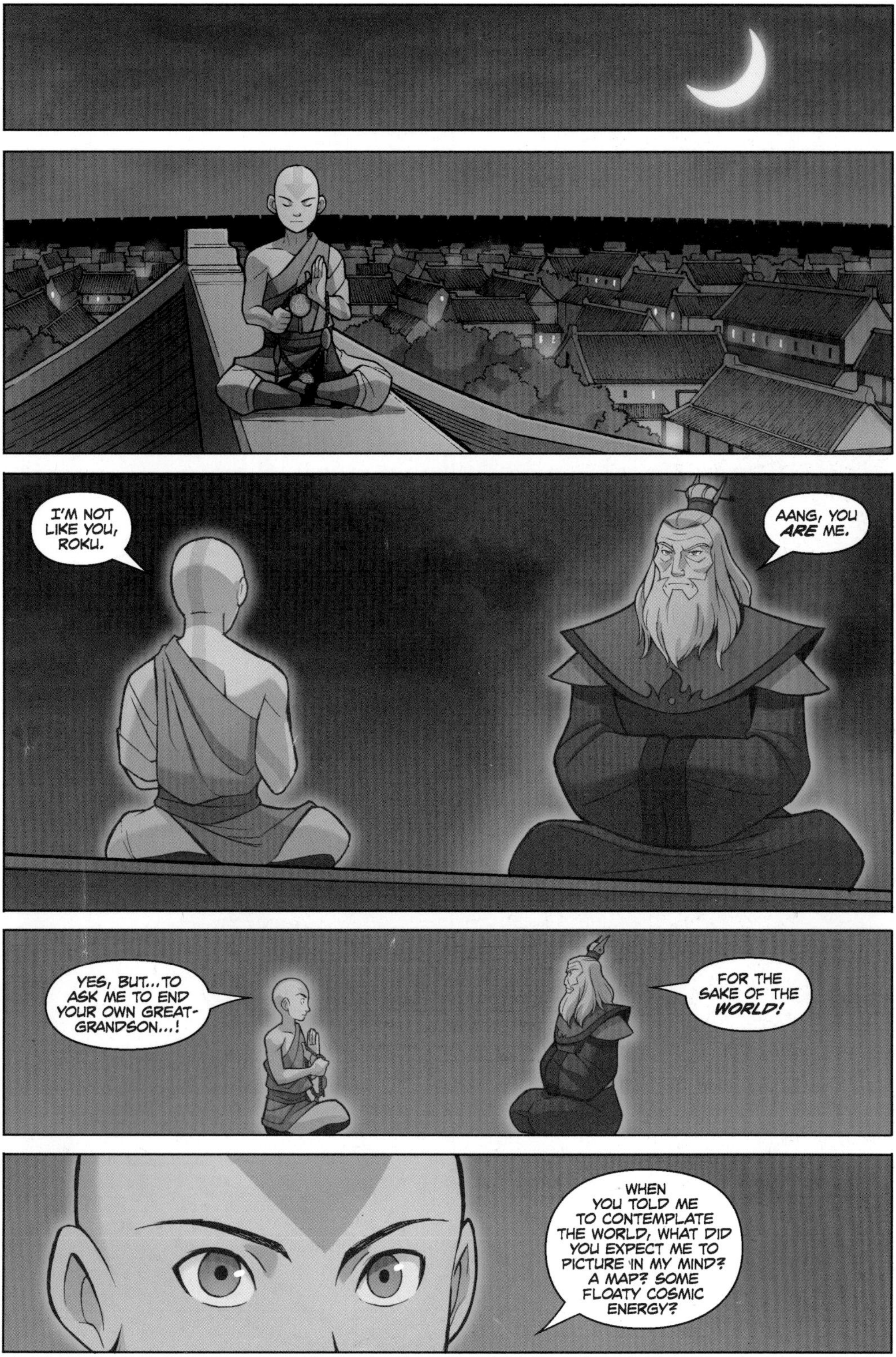
I'M NOT LIKE YOU, ROKU.
AANG, YOU *ARE* ME.
YES, BUT...TO ASK ME TO END YOUR OWN GREAT-GRANDSON...!
FOR THE SAKE OF THE *WORLD!*
WHEN YOU TOLD ME TO CONTEMPLATE THE WORLD, WHAT DID YOU EXPECT ME TO PICTURE IN MY MIND? A MAP? SOME FLOATY COSMIC ENERGY?

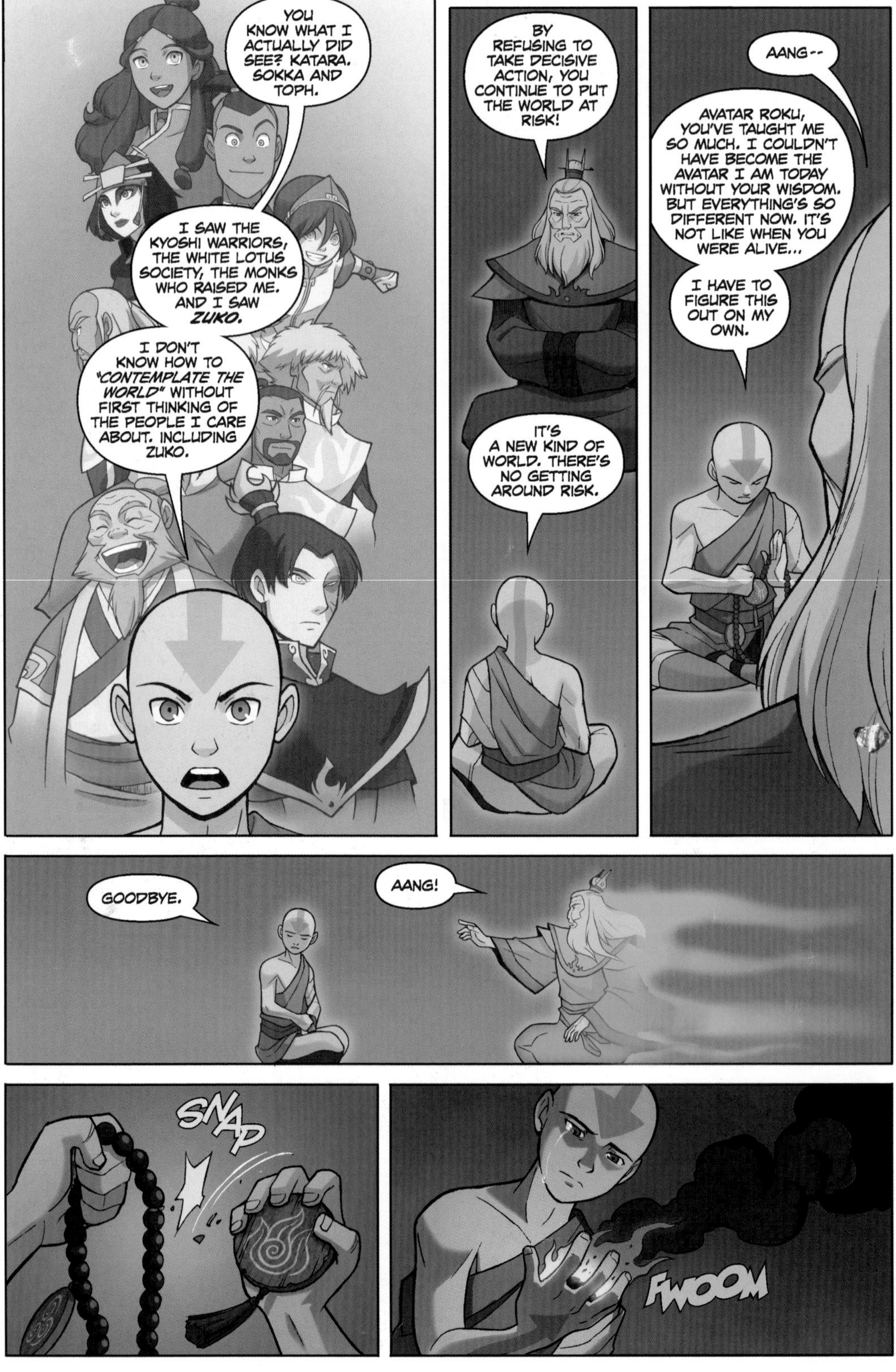
YOU KNOW WHAT I ACTUALLY DID SEE? KATARA. SOKKA AND TOPH.
I SAW THE KYOSHI WARRIORS, THE WHITE LOTUS SOCIETY, THE MONKS WHO RAISED ME. AND I SAW *ZUKO.*
I DON'T KNOW HOW TO *"CONTEMPLATE THE WORLD"* WITHOUT FIRST THINKING OF THE PEOPLE I CARE ABOUT. INCLUDING ZUKO.
BY REFUSING TO TAKE DECISIVE ACTION, YOU CONTINUE TO PUT THE WORLD AT RISK!
IT'S A NEW KIND OF WORLD. THERE'S NO GETTING AROUND RISK.
AANG--
AVATAR ROKU, YOU'VE TAUGHT ME SO MUCH. I COULDN'T HAVE BECOME THE AVATAR I AM TODAY WITHOUT YOUR WISDOM. BUT EVERYTHING'S SO DIFFERENT NOW. IT'S NOT LIKE WHEN YOU WERE ALIVE...
I HAVE TO FIGURE THIS OUT ON MY OWN.
GOODBYE.
AANG!
SNAP
FWOOM

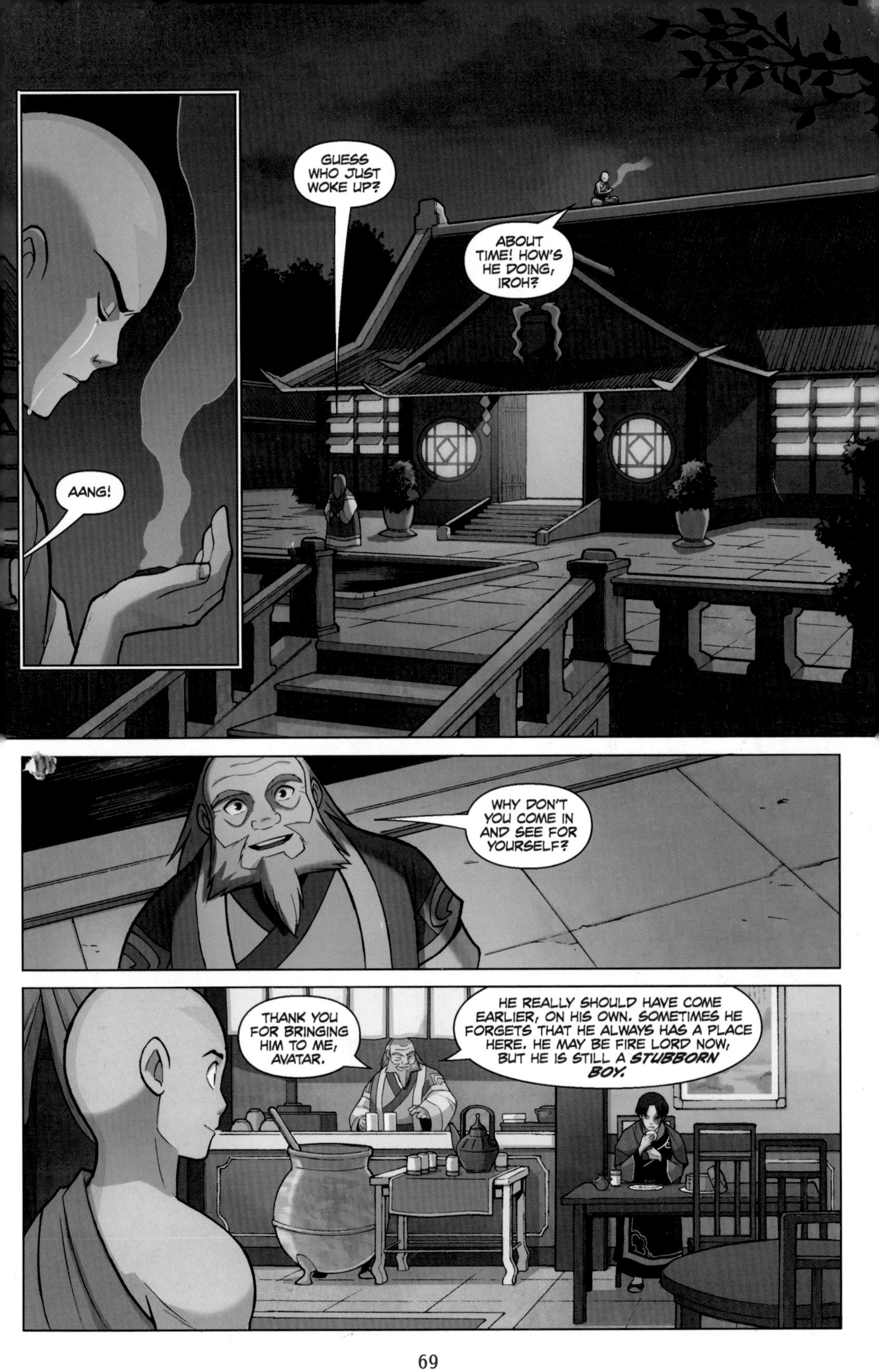
GUESS WHO JUST WOKE UP?
ABOUT TIME! HOW'S HE DOING, IROH?
AANG!
WHY DON'T YOU COME IN AND SEE FOR YOURSELF?
THANK YOU FOR BRINGING HIM TO ME, AVATAR.
HE REALLY SHOULD HAVE COME EARLIER, ON HIS OWN. SOMETIMES HE FORGETS THAT HE ALWAYS HAS A PLACE HERE. HE MAY BE FIRE LORD NOW, BUT HE IS STILL A *STUBBORN BOY.*

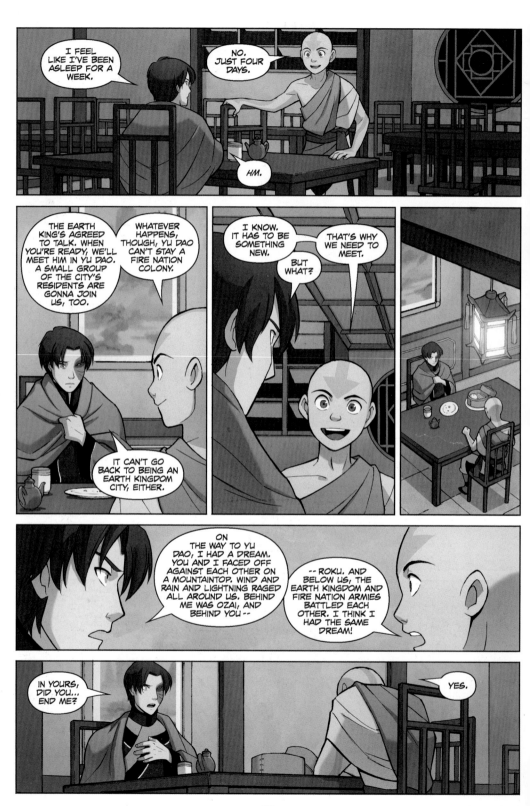

I FEEL LIKE I'VE BEEN ASLEEP FOR A WEEK.

NO. JUST FOUR DAYS.

HM.

THE EARTH KING'S AGREED TO TALK. WHEN YOU'RE READY, WE'LL MEET HIM IN YU DAO. A SMALL GROUP OF THE CITY'S RESIDENTS ARE GONNA JOIN US, TOO.

WHATEVER HAPPENS, THOUGH, YU DAO CAN'T STAY A FIRE NATION COLONY.

IT CAN'T GO BACK TO BEING AN EARTH KINGDOM CITY, EITHER.

I KNOW. IT HAS TO BE SOMETHING NEW.

BUT WHAT?

THAT'S WHY WE NEED TO MEET.

ON THE WAY TO YU DAO, I HAD A DREAM. YOU AND I FACED OFF AGAINST EACH OTHER ON A MOUNTAINTOP. WIND AND RAIN AND LIGHTNING RAGED ALL AROUND US. BEHIND ME WAS OZAI, AND BEHIND YOU --

-- ROKU. AND BELOW US, THE EARTH KINGDOM AND FIRE NATION ARMIES BATTLED EACH OTHER. I THINK I HAD THE SAME DREAM!

IN YOURS, DID YOU... END ME?

YES.

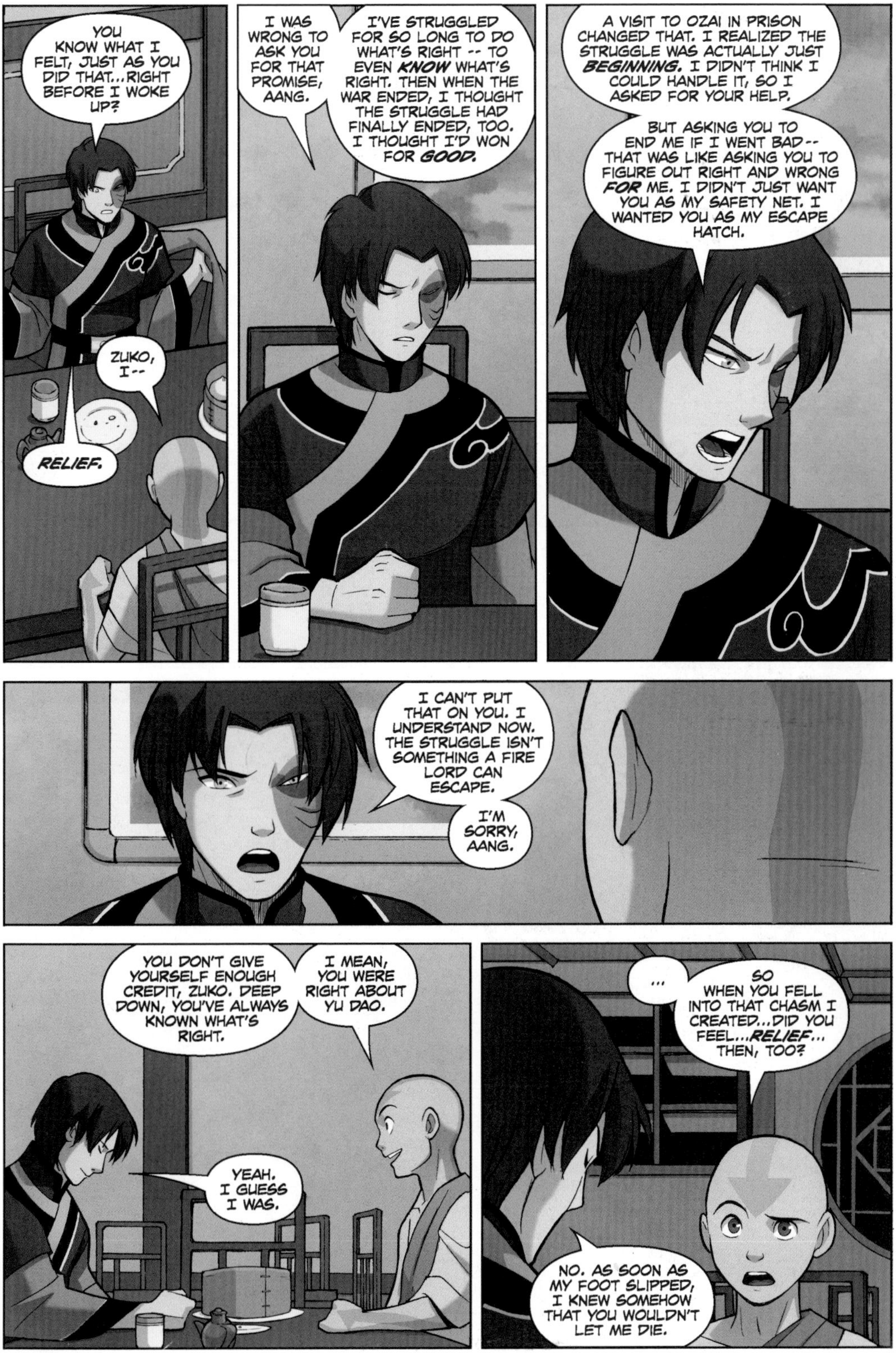

YOU KNOW WHAT I FELT, JUST AS YOU DID THAT...RIGHT BEFORE I WOKE UP?
ZUKO, I--
RELIEF.
I WAS WRONG TO ASK YOU FOR THAT PROMISE, AANG.
I'VE STRUGGLED FOR SO LONG TO DO WHAT'S RIGHT -- TO EVEN KNOW WHAT'S RIGHT. THEN WHEN THE WAR ENDED, I THOUGHT THE STRUGGLE HAD FINALLY ENDED, TOO. I THOUGHT I'D WON FOR GOOD.
A VISIT TO OZAI IN PRISON CHANGED THAT. I REALIZED THE STRUGGLE WAS ACTUALLY JUST BEGINNING. I DIDN'T THINK I COULD HANDLE IT, SO I ASKED FOR YOUR HELP.
BUT ASKING YOU TO END ME IF I WENT BAD--THAT WAS LIKE ASKING YOU TO FIGURE OUT RIGHT AND WRONG FOR ME. I DIDN'T JUST WANT YOU AS MY SAFETY NET. I WANTED YOU AS MY ESCAPE HATCH.
I CAN'T PUT THAT ON YOU. I UNDERSTAND NOW. THE STRUGGLE ISN'T SOMETHING A FIRE LORD CAN ESCAPE.
I'M SORRY, AANG.
YOU DON'T GIVE YOURSELF ENOUGH CREDIT, ZUKO. DEEP DOWN, YOU'VE ALWAYS KNOWN WHAT'S RIGHT.
I MEAN, YOU WERE RIGHT ABOUT YU DAO.
YEAH. I GUESS I WAS.
...
SO WHEN YOU FELL INTO THAT CHASM I CREATED...DID YOU FEEL...RELIEF... THEN, TOO?
NO. AS SOON AS MY FOOT SLIPPED, I KNEW SOMEHOW THAT YOU WOULDN'T LET ME DIE.

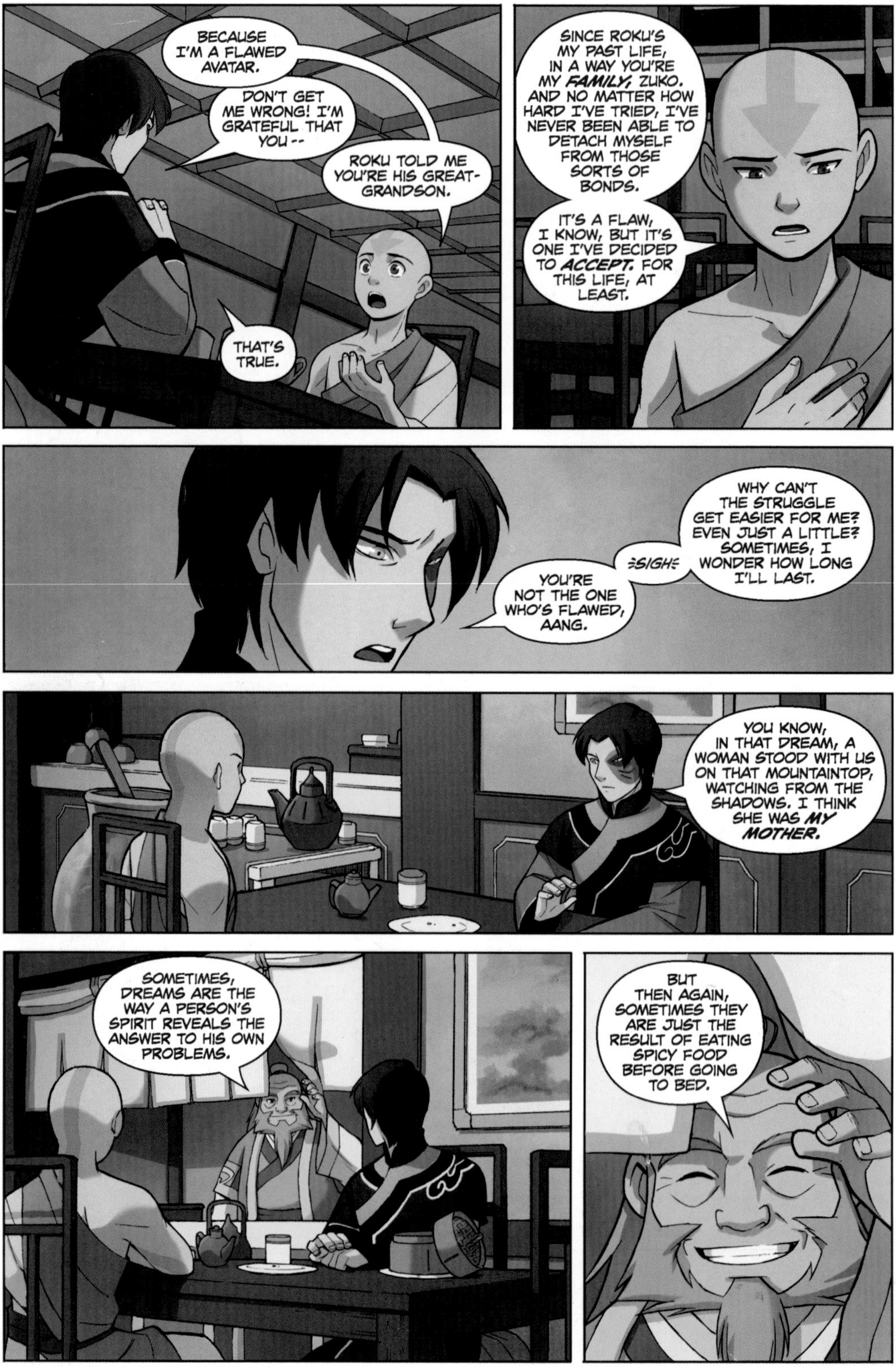
BECAUSE I'M A FLAWED AVATAR.
DON'T GET ME WRONG! I'M GRATEFUL THAT YOU --
ROKU TOLD ME YOU'RE HIS GREAT-GRANDSON.
THAT'S TRUE.
SINCE ROKU'S MY PAST LIFE, IN A WAY YOU'RE MY FAMILY, ZUKO. AND NO MATTER HOW HARD I'VE TRIED, I'VE NEVER BEEN ABLE TO DETACH MYSELF FROM THOSE SORTS OF BONDS.
IT'S A FLAW, I KNOW, BUT IT'S ONE I'VE DECIDED TO ACCEPT. FOR THIS LIFE, AT LEAST.
YOU'RE NOT THE ONE WHO'S FLAWED, AANG.
SIGH
WHY CAN'T THE STRUGGLE GET EASIER FOR ME? EVEN JUST A LITTLE? SOMETIMES, I WONDER HOW LONG I'LL LAST.
YOU KNOW, IN THAT DREAM, A WOMAN STOOD WITH US ON THAT MOUNTAINTOP, WATCHING FROM THE SHADOWS. I THINK SHE WAS MY MOTHER.
SOMETIMES, DREAMS ARE THE WAY A PERSON'S SPIRIT REVEALS THE ANSWER TO HIS OWN PROBLEMS.
BUT THEN AGAIN, SOMETIMES THEY ARE JUST THE RESULT OF EATING SPICY FOOD BEFORE GOING TO BED.

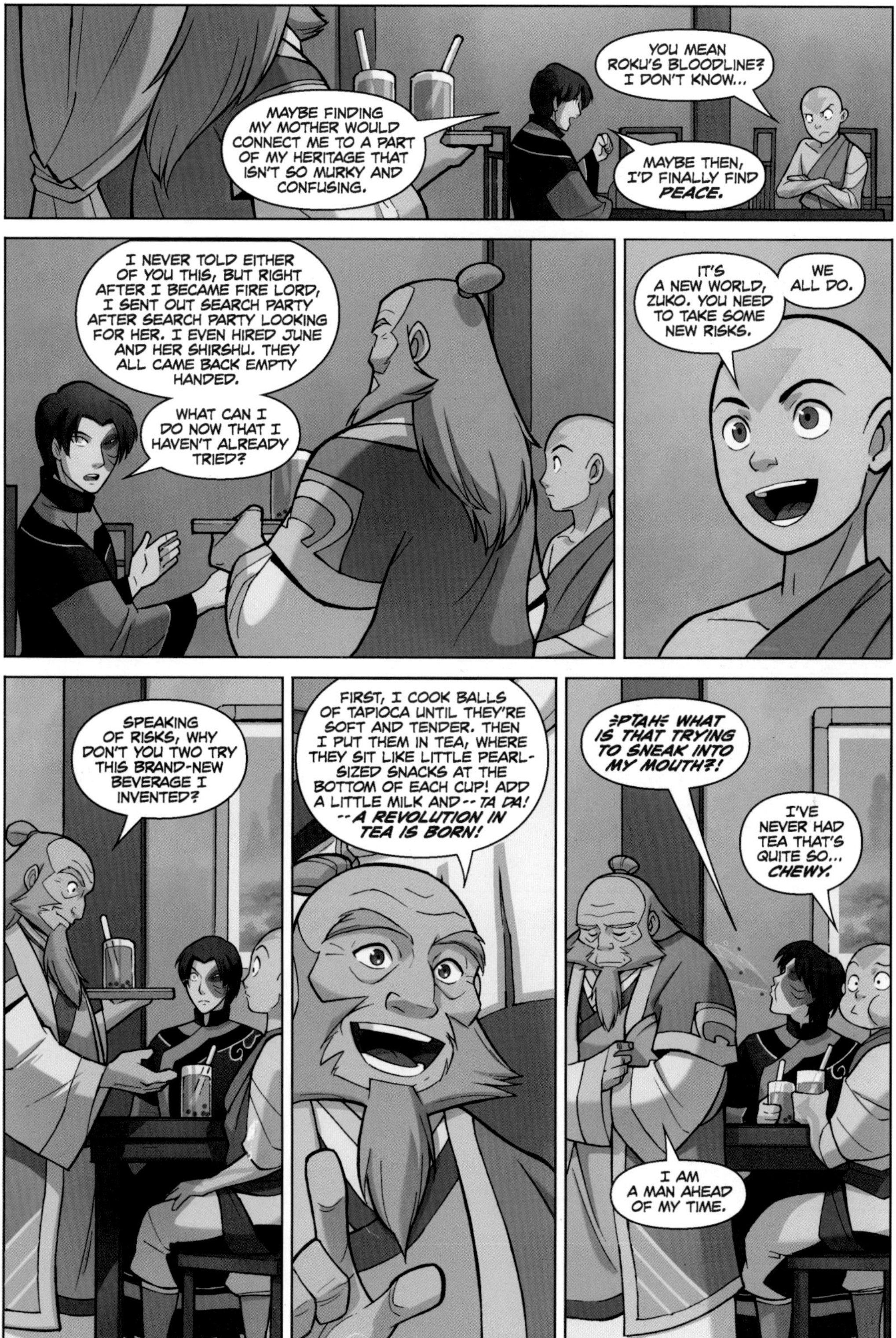
MAYBE FINDING MY MOTHER WOULD CONNECT ME TO A PART OF MY HERITAGE THAT ISN'T SO MURKY AND CONFUSING.
YOU MEAN ROKU'S BLOODLINE? I DON'T KNOW...
MAYBE THEN, I'D FINALLY FIND PEACE.
I NEVER TOLD EITHER OF YOU THIS, BUT RIGHT AFTER I BECAME FIRE LORD, I SENT OUT SEARCH PARTY AFTER SEARCH PARTY LOOKING FOR HER. I EVEN HIRED JUNE AND HER SHIRSHU. THEY ALL CAME BACK EMPTY HANDED.
WHAT CAN I DO NOW THAT I HAVEN'T ALREADY TRIED?
IT'S A NEW WORLD, ZUKO. YOU NEED TO TAKE SOME NEW RISKS.
WE ALL DO.
SPEAKING OF RISKS, WHY DON'T YOU TWO TRY THIS BRAND-NEW BEVERAGE I INVENTED?
FIRST, I COOK BALLS OF TAPIOCA UNTIL THEY'RE SOFT AND TENDER. THEN I PUT THEM IN TEA, WHERE THEY SIT LIKE LITTLE PEARL-SIZED SNACKS AT THE BOTTOM OF EACH CUP! ADD A LITTLE MILK AND--TA DA! --A REVOLUTION IN TEA IS BORN!
PTAH! WHAT IS THAT TRYING TO SNEAK INTO MY MOUTH?!
I'VE NEVER HAD TEA THAT'S QUITE SO... CHEWY.
I AM A MAN AHEAD OF MY TIME.

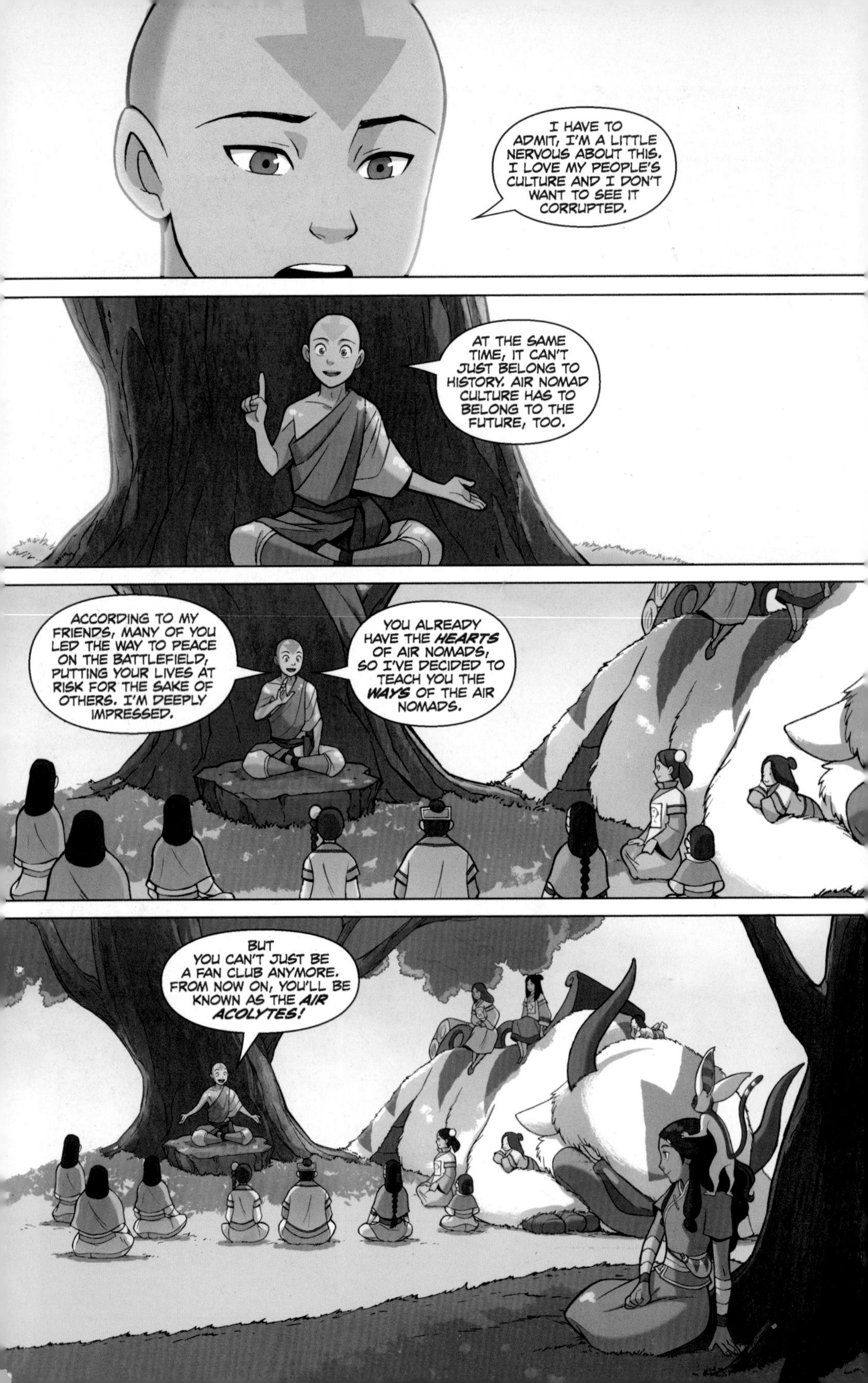
I HAVE TO ADMIT, I'M A LITTLE NERVOUS ABOUT THIS. I LOVE MY PEOPLE'S CULTURE AND I DON'T WANT TO SEE IT CORRUPTED.
AT THE SAME TIME, IT CAN'T JUST BELONG TO HISTORY. AIR NOMAD CULTURE HAS TO BELONG TO THE FUTURE, TOO.
ACCORDING TO MY FRIENDS, MANY OF YOU LED THE WAY TO PEACE ON THE BATTLEFIELD, PUTTING YOUR LIVES AT RISK FOR THE SAKE OF OTHERS. I'M DEEPLY IMPRESSED.
YOU ALREADY HAVE THE ***HEARTS*** OF AIR NOMADS, SO I'VE DECIDED TO TEACH YOU THE ***WAYS*** OF THE AIR NOMADS.
BUT YOU CAN'T JUST BE A FAN CLUB ANYMORE. FROM NOW ON, YOU'LL BE KNOWN AS THE ***AIR ACOLYTES!***

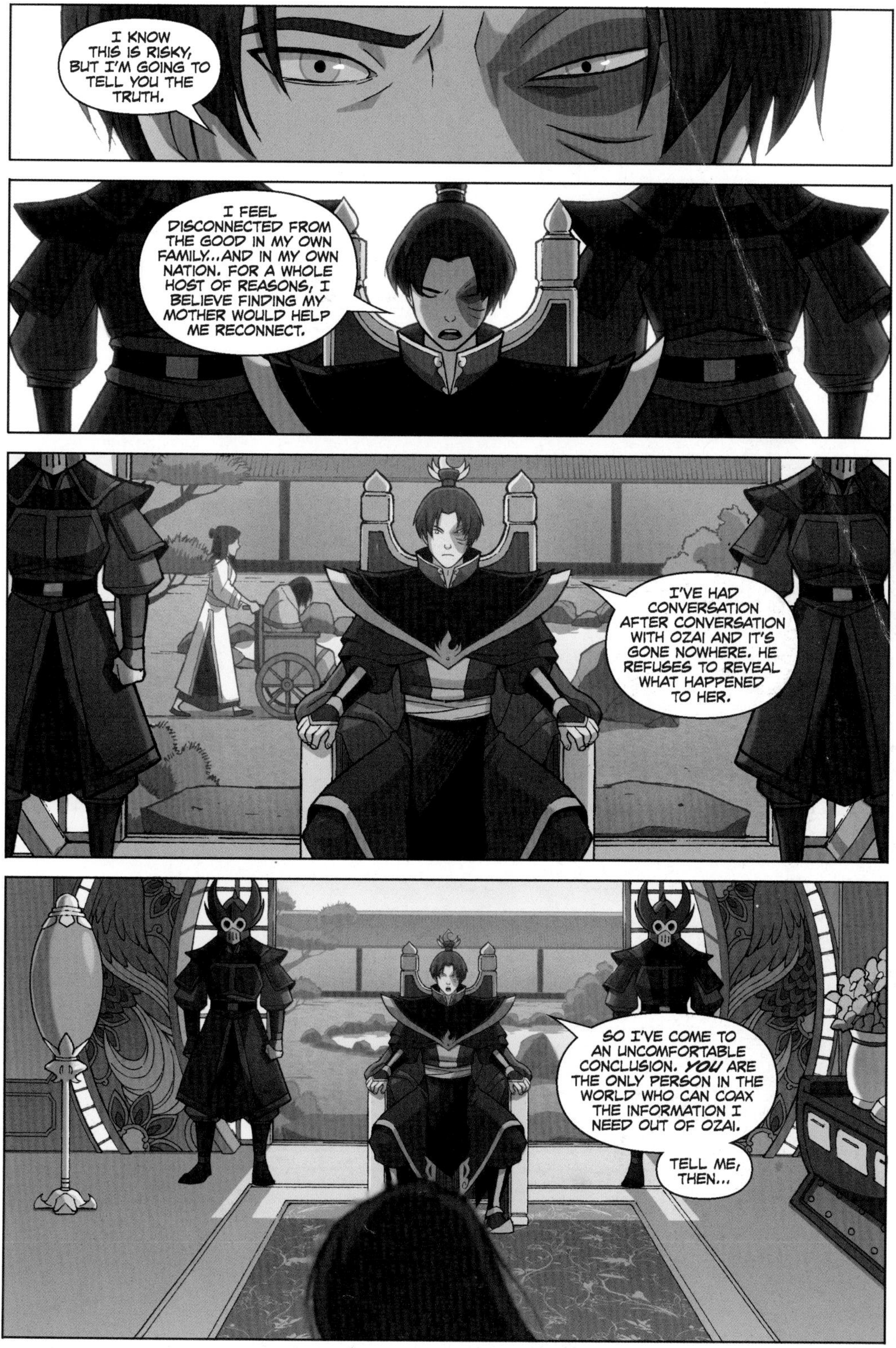
I KNOW THIS IS RISKY, BUT I'M GOING TO TELL YOU THE TRUTH.
I FEEL DISCONNECTED FROM THE GOOD IN MY OWN FAMILY...AND IN MY OWN NATION. FOR A WHOLE HOST OF REASONS, I BELIEVE FINDING MY MOTHER WOULD HELP ME RECONNECT.
I'VE HAD CONVERSATION AFTER CONVERSATION WITH OZAI AND IT'S GONE NOWHERE. HE REFUSES TO REVEAL WHAT HAPPENED TO HER.
SO I'VE COME TO AN UNCOMFORTABLE CONCLUSION. *YOU* ARE THE ONLY PERSON IN THE WORLD WHO CAN COAX THE INFORMATION I NEED OUT OF OZAI.
TELL ME, THEN...

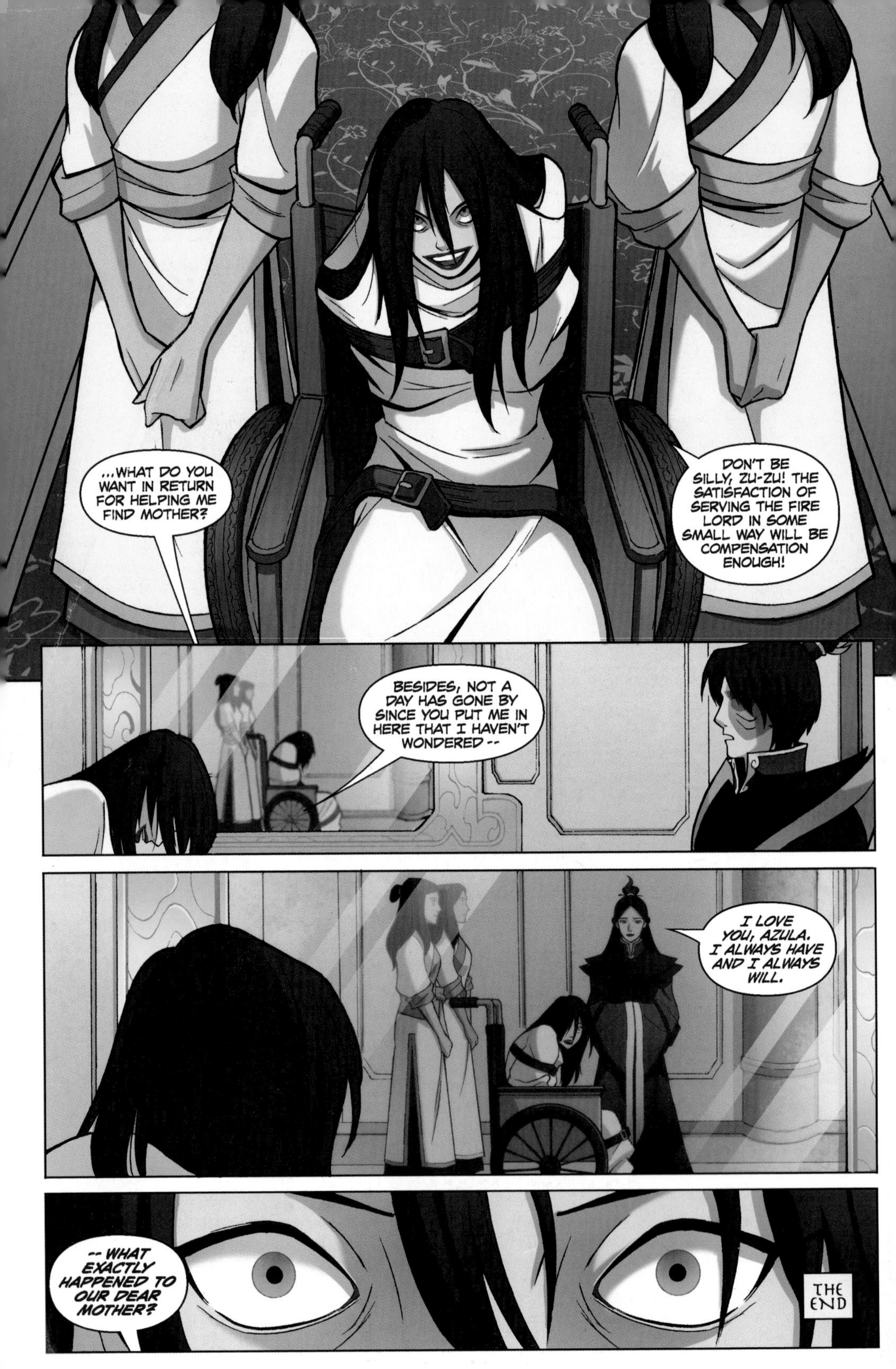
...WHAT DO YOU WANT IN RETURN FOR HELPING ME FIND MOTHER?
DON'T BE SILLY, ZU-ZU! THE SATISFACTION OF SERVING THE FIRE LORD IN SOME SMALL WAY WILL BE COMPENSATION ENOUGH!
BESIDES, NOT A DAY HAS GONE BY SINCE YOU PUT ME IN HERE THAT I HAVEN'T WONDERED --
I LOVE YOU, AZULA. I ALWAYS HAVE AND I ALWAYS WILL.
-- WHAT EXACTLY HAPPENED TO OUR DEAR MOTHER?
THE END

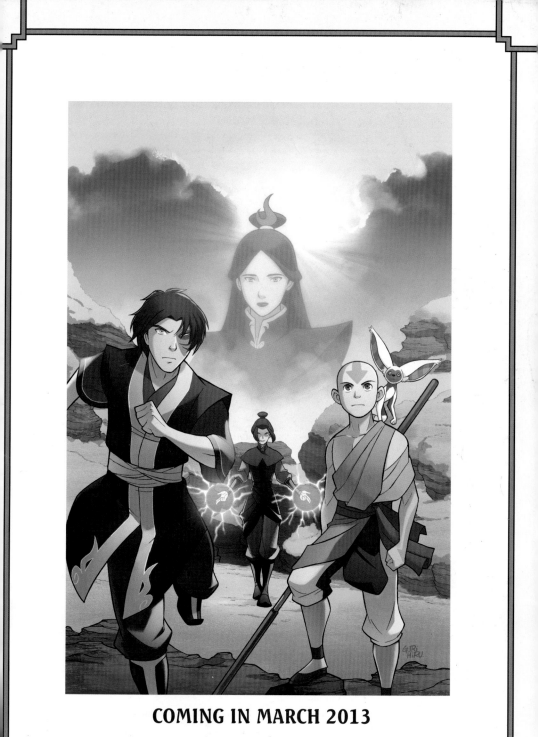

COMING IN MARCH 2013

Fire Lord Zuko's quest to find his mother begins in . . .

THE SEARCH · PART ONE

ALSO AVAILABLE FROM DARK HORSE BOOKS

nickelodeon
AVATAR
THE LAST AIRBENDER
THE LOST ADVENTURES

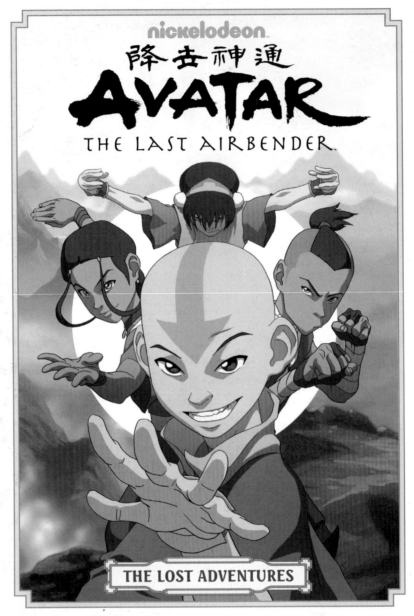

Twenty-eight stories set during the original three seasons, including over seventy pages of never-before-seen comics!

AVAILABLE AT YOUR LOCAL COMICS SHOP OR BOOKSTORE

To find a comics shop in your area, call 1-888-266-4226
For more information or to order direct, visit DarkHorse.com or call 1-800-862-0052